LIVING
IN THE
SON

Kyle + Amber,

Coram Deo!

Wade R...

Kyle + Amber

Orem Deo!

[signature]

LIVING

IN THE

SON

50 ESSENTIAL
PASSAGES AND MEDITATIONS
FROM THE NEW TESTAMENT

WADE ROBINSON

LIVING IN THE SON© 2014 Wade Robinson All Rights Reserved.

Scriptures taken from the Holy Bible, New International Version®, NIV®Copyright © 1973, 1978, 1984, 2011 by Biblica Inc®Used by permission. All rights reserved worldwide.

ISBN PRINT 978-0-9892440-9-1

Book Cover Design by Estela Jia Ceyril Redulla
Front Cover Photo Courtesy of 123rf.com/Vasily Pindyurin
Back Cover Author Photo by Ronnie Sweet | Sweet Reflections Photography
Interior Layout Design by Sarah ONeal | evecustomartwork.com

To order this book, please visit CondeoPress.com

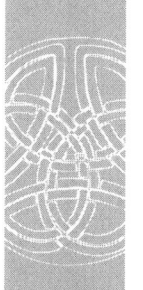

ACKNOWLEDGEMENTS

To my amazing wife Kristie and my five wonderful kids for their love and support. Thank you for being so much more than I could have ever asked for or expected from God!

Special thanks to Cherylann Dozier and Linda Lackey, who did a wonderful job giving feedback and editing the text.

CONTENTS

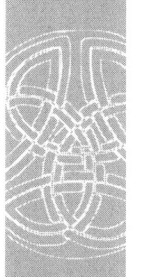

Introduction	i
Using This Devotional	v
The Word Became Flesh	1
Gabriel's Messages	7
The Birth of Jesus	13
John The Baptist	19
Jesus' Baptism and Temptation	25
The Sermon On The Mount, Part 1	31
The Sermon On The Mount, Part 2	37
The Kingdom of Heaven	43
The Good Samaritan	49
Lost and Found	55
Feeding The Five Thousand	61
Walking On Water	67
Healing A Blind Man	73
Healing A Possessed Man	79
Raising Lazarus	85
The Last Supper	91
Arrest and Trial	97
The Crucifixion	103
The Resurrection	109
The Ascension	115
The Day of Pentecost	121
Growth and Persecution	127

The First Martyr	133
Sharing the Word	139
Good News For All	145
The Road To Damascus	151
The First Missionary Journey	157
The Council at Jerusalem	163
Missionary Journeys	169
The Trial Before Festus	175
More Than Conquerors	181
Fruit of the Spirit	187
The Armor of God	193
Rejoice In The Lord	199
The Supremacy of Christ	205
Elders and Deacons	211
The Love of Money	217
Good Soldiers of Christ	223
Scripture is God-Breathed	229
The Second Coming of Christ	235
The Most Excellent Way	241
A New Creation in Christ	247
A Living Hope	253
Faith and Works	259
Love One Another	265
A Voice and a Vision	271
Messages to the Churches	277
The Throne Room of Heaven	283
Hallelujah!	289
The New Jerusalem	295
Endnotes	**301**

INTRODUCTION

This is what the Sovereign Lord, the Holy One of Israel, says: "In repentance and rest is your salvation, in quietness and trust is your strength, but you would have none of it."
Isaiah 30:15

Years ago I heard a speaker talk about small groups. I don't remember much of what he said honestly, but he used an illustration that has stayed with me ever since. He held up a big zip-lock bag filled with puzzle pieces. He said that the typical person spends his life collecting little puzzle pieces of information, which he stores in his bag but never actually fits together. He truly enjoys the "aha" moments of discovery. But he just keeps collecting pieces of truth and wisdom and then putting them into his bag with all the others. His motto might be, "The one with the most pieces wins!"

His illustration worked for me on a number of different levels. First, I love collecting tidbits of knowledge and wisdom. I have a nearly insatiable hunger for information. It became so insatiable that it became a problem in my life. I thought that something magical would happen when I finally collected enough information on how to be a good husband, or a great father, or successful in my career. But as my information pieces continued to accumulate it only led to a greater level of anxiety and sense of failure. The more bits of knowledge, or puzzle pieces, that I collected the fuller my bag got but the heavier they all weighed on me. Each little piece seemed to have its own little voice that kept nagging me about what I should be doing. It led to an ever-growing chorus of discontent that kept telling me more and more loudly that I was not doing enough. Ever.

Second, I realized instinctively that a person can't put the pieces together without having a picture to start with. Puzzle pieces are a part of a bigger picture. The big picture that I think we are all trying to piece together is what we might call "The Answer to the Puzzle of Life." What is life all about? If you were to look on the cover of that box what or who do you think would be on it? Personally, I am pretty sure that it is a portrait of Jesus Christ. Jesus said himself that he was "the Way, the Truth and the Life."[1] You can't get more ultimate in answering the puzzle of life than that!

I believe that the picture on the front of "The Answer to the Puzzle of Life" box is a vibrant, dramatic, gorgeously colored, heart-wrenching, panorama of Jesus' life and work that Vincent Van Gogh might have painted on his very best day; something on the scale of Michelangelo's Sistine Chapel. Imagine getting all of that into a jigsaw puzzle.

Accepting that "the answer to the puzzle of life" is Jesus Christ makes all the difference in the world. It leads me to the belief that the more we construct our picture of his life and work the greater our ability will be to understand and navigate through life. *The more fully we see him the more prepared we will be to live life.* There are countless things that people can pursue in life, but if Jesus Christ is the answer to it all, is there anything more important than understanding who he is and what he has done?

I believe that we are meant to live in the reality of who Jesus is and what he has done for us. In essence we are meant to live in the Son, in the light of his life and work. As the Apostle Paul said, "For God, who said, 'Let light shine out of darkness,' made his light shine in our hearts to give us the light of the knowledge of God's glory displayed in the face of Christ." He is the subject, the center, the explanation, the point of all of Scripture and history (Luke 24:25-27). As we learn to gaze within our hearts at the ever-growing portrait that Scripture gives us of Jesus Christ we can appreciate him in as much detail as we have and learn to long for more. It is this growing appreciation for him, and what we can have in him, which gets closest to describing the source of Christian joy (Nehemiah 8:10; Psalm 16:11; Philippians).

Gazing on him though depends on our willingness to *slow down* and learn to fit His Biblical insights into place with as much patience, watchfulness and stillness as we can muster; which brings us back to our puzzle illustration. *The "end" of the puzzle* for a Christian is not the anxious effort to finish placing all of our pieces into the puzzle as quickly as we can (and then push the puzzle off to the side before putting it back in its box): it is *accepting the process* by which we come to deeply know and appreciate the subject of it all: Jesus Christ!

Seeing the process of knowing him in terms of our jigsaw puzzle illustration helps us see how our experience of God can grow as we look *through the puzzle* we are constructing at the Person it is revealing. As we find and fit pieces into our picture of Jesus' life and work, we benefit by taking the time to remember when we first discovered the pieces we have. We benefit by remembering the "yes!" moments of satisfaction when they clicked into place. And we benefit when we step back and admire the One who provided the pieces and embodies the pieces and sometimes speaks to us through those pieces.

Gazing into our ever growing picture of Jesus Christ, within the frame of Scripture, leads to the ultimate pursuit of our lives: living *for* the Son, Jesus Christ.[2] The vast majority of Christians know that they are to live *for* Jesus Christ; reflecting his life and sharing his message with others. Yet so many skip past the "step" that makes that life possible--gazing on and glorying in Christ himself; or to put it another way, living in adoration of the Son. This is what makes him real and present to us. It is our ongoing, deepening response to who he is and what he has done for us and all of mankind that propels us forward in the Christian life. Looking adoringly upon the Son helps us live *in the Son*! And it is living *in* the Son that moves us to want to live *for* the Son.

We need the "aha" moments of discovery. We need the "yes" moments of connection. But neither will ever be enough to satisfy our soul! We were created to be filled by a person: God himself. He alone is enough to fill our soul's hunger. He alone, in His real presence in our life, provides the Shalom peace, love and joy for which we long. And God in all his glory comes to us as we look upon His Son, Jesus Christ. My prayer is that this devotional encourages our adoration of Jesus and enlarges His place in our life. *Coram Deo!*

USING THIS DEVOTIONAL

The fifty meditations in this book are based on the fifty New Testament readings from *The Essential 100 Bible Challenge* program from Scripture Union.³ I have added personal reflections on each passage as well as correlation verses that illuminate the readings. I have also included nine prayers and the Apostle's Creed to these readings. The Creed and prayers are included to strengthen your rootedness in the Scriptural and Christian tradition we have been gifted with.

This devotional is structured to help you learn to slow down, read and reflect on the text, appreciate what the text adds to your understanding, and then pause to *look through the text at the Son*. Once you have paused to see the Son in your mind's eye, patiently listen for God's still small voice, and then walk through your day with an awareness of his immediate presence in your life. There is much to learn about this process, but I hope that you are benefited from the resources that have been brought together in this devotional.

Gazing on the Son through Scripture prepares you to hear God speak to you. One of the strongest threads through Scripture is the truth that *God Speaks*; and it is my firm conviction that He did not cease speaking with the completion of the New Testament. You may have experienced Him speaking in ways that you may not have recognized at the time. Have you ever had a sudden insight, a clear sense of conviction, a word of reassurance or a piece of guidance when you were worshiping or learning something in Scripture? These are all ways that God continues to speak to us through His Word, Jesus Christ, today.[4]

I hope this devotional helps you collect and click in a few new or long-held puzzle pieces. Each passage has untold numbers of pieces. Don't get too concerned, though, about the amount you get each time. Know that as you learn to practice patience, watchfulness and stillness before God you can develop the discipline of seeing and savoring Jesus through Scripture. Ask the Holy Spirit to enlighten and guide you in this process, accepting that it will be in His own way and time. Let Him be in control!

How can you make the most of this devotional?[5]

- Listen to or read the full passage in a translation of your choice. *The Essential 100 Challenge* has audio files of all the passages that you can purchase.

- *Slowly* re-read the section of the passage provided in the devotional. Be patient and watchful as you chew on each word and phrase. After you have read the passage, go back and highlight or underline any key words or phrases that stand out to you. Do not worry about marking up the Scripture passage: this is why we have included it.

- Pause and prayerfully enter into a state of stillness and silence. Do not try to rush this or make yourself feel anything. Remind yourself that you are in the immediate presence of Christ. He sits on His throne ready to be approached by you.

- Listen for any words, either from the text or otherwise, that come to your mind as you pray. Circle or write down these words. What might they mean to you? Where might they play out in your life today?

- Read the Reflection and Correlation verses for the passage. They are purposely short and suggestive. Look to Christ in your mind's eye and lift him up in praise.

- Recite the prayer or Creed given for each meditation out loud to God. The nine prayers and the Apostle's Creed are in the same order throughout the book so that by the end you will recite each one five times.

- As you go through your day, meditate on the words that came to mind during your reflection time. Linger on them even if they make no immediate sense to you. *Remind yourself often of the fact that you are living in the presence of Christ.*

God can speak to you through Scripture. He can speak through a still, small voice that lightly brings a word, or truth, or person, or piece of advice to mind. There is nothing uniquely different about you that keeps him from "getting through." It is essential though to begin practicing daily confession before God. Have you acknowledged all your known sins to him without any excuses or explanations? Have you asked him to search your heart for anything you need to change?

Journal your experiences. Write down the key words and images that come to mind. Add any questions you have or areas of further study that you might want to follow up on.

One last word: there is a danger in seeking to experience God through Scripture in this way. There is a trial-and-error aspect to learning this skill. Depending on your personal background and depth of study in Scripture you could "hear" God leading you in a direction that is against the clear teachings of *His* Scripture! God will never lead you to do something He has clearly taught to be sin. As you open yourself up to hearing God through His Word it is vital to be in accountable relationships with other growing Christians who can be sounding-boards and safe-guards along the way. The reward is well worth the risk, but it is imperative that we stay open to the feedback of Christians who have walked with the Lord and weathered more of life than we have!

The Word Became Flesh

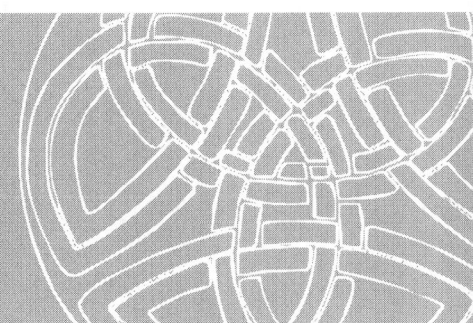

Passage: John 1:1-18[6]

Meditation: John 1:1-18
Pause and Reflect Silently
Highlight Key Phrases
Look to and Lift up Christ

¹*In the beginning was the Word, and the Word was with God, and the Word was God.* ²*He was with God in the beginning.*

³*Through him all things were made; without him nothing was made that has been made.* ⁴*In him was life, and that life was the light of all mankind.* ⁵*The light shines in the darkness, and the darkness has not overcome it.*

⁶*There was a man sent from God whose name was John.* ⁷*He came as a witness to testify concerning that light, so that through him all might believe.* ⁸*He himself was not the light; he came only as a witness to the light.*

⁹*The true light that gives light to everyone was coming into the world.* ¹⁰*He was in the world, and though the world was made through him, the world did not recognize him.* ¹¹*He came to that which was his own, but his own did not receive him.*

¹²*Yet to all who did receive him, to those who believed in his*

name, he gave the right to become children of God—[13]children born not of natural descent, nor of human decision or a husband's will, but born of God.

[14]The Word became flesh and made his dwelling among us. We have seen his glory, the glory of the one and only Son, who came from the Father, full of grace and truth.

[15]John testified concerning him. He cried out, saying, "This is the one I spoke about when I said, 'He who comes after me has surpassed me because he was before me.'"

[16]Out of his fullness we have all received grace in place of grace already given. [17]For the law was given through Moses; grace and truth came through Jesus Christ.

[18]No one has ever seen God, but the one and only Son, who is himself God and is in closest relationship with the Father, has made him known.

REFLECTION

John opens his gospel on a cosmic level by introducing Jesus as the Word of God. "In the beginning" recalls the opening words of Genesis 1:1: "In the beginning God created the heavens and the earth." God created the universe through His Word ("God spoke").

"Word" here is the Greek *logos*, which had several meanings. Ordinarily it referred to a spoken word. In Greek thought,[7] *logos* referred to the rational principle, or "world-soul," that created, brought order and permeates the entire universe. It was viewed as a creative power that held great wisdom for people. Stoic philosophers held that the Logos was what made everything in the universe understandable.

Scripture tells us that God's Word is creative in its power: "By the word of the Lord were the heavens made, their starry host by the breath of his mouth" (Psalm 33:6). In Jewish usage, "Word" came to be used as a synonym for God.[8]

John is saying that the "Word" of God is not just a power or a principle behind the universe but that it is a Divine Person: Jesus Christ Himself. And as the Word, Jesus communicates what God is like "inside Himself." When we see Jesus we see the true nature and heart of God. Further, when John says, "the Word was with God" the Greek can be translated "The Word was *toward* God." Everything Jesus did was centered on and done for His Father.

Jesus, the divine God-man, was witnessed to by one of the most famous men of the time: John the Baptist. John was a revered prophet and *his word* about someone went a long way! One of the great tragedies of Jesus' life, though, is that the Jewish people of his time did not recognize who he was. They had been divinely taught and prepared to receive their Messiah but when he arrived they ultimately rejected and crucified him.

CORRELATION

For by [Jesus Christ] all things were created: things in heaven and on earth, visible and invisible, whether thrones or powers or rulers or authorities; all things were created by him and for him. He is before all things, and in him all things hold together.
     Colossians 1:16

The Son is the radiance of God's glory and the exact representation of his being, sustaining all things by his powerful word. After he had provided purification for sins, he sat down at the right hand of the Majesty in heaven.
     Hebrews 1:3

RECITATION

Lord, you have been our dwelling place throughout all generations.

Before the mountains were born or you brought forth the universe, from everlasting to everlasting, you are God.

Forgive us our sins that we might not be consumed by your anger.

Teach us to number our days that we may gain a heart of wisdom.

Satisfy us in the morning with your unfailing love, that we may sing for joy and be glad in all our days.

Heal us and restore us from our afflictions, Lord, for this world is filled with many troubles.

May your favor rest upon us, and may the work of our hands be established by you, Father.[9]

A prayer based on Psalm 90

APPLICATION

What has come to mind, either through the passage or in your reflection that you want to remember?

Gabriel's Messages

Passage: Luke 1:1-66

Meditation: Luke 1:46-66
Pause and Reflect Silently
Highlight Key Phrases
Look to and Lift up Christ

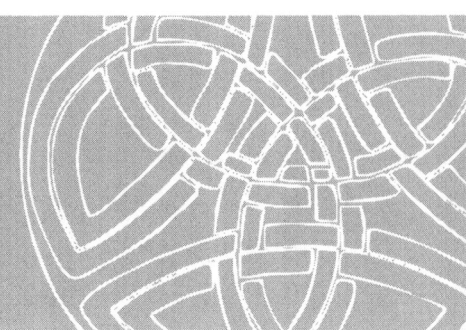

⁴⁶ *And Mary said:*

> "My soul glorifies the Lord
>   ⁴⁷ and my spirit rejoices in God my Savior,
> ⁴⁸ for he has been mindful
>   of the humble state of his servant.
> From now on all generations will call me blessed,
>   ⁴⁹ for the Mighty One has done great things for me—
>   holy is his name.
> ⁵⁰ His mercy extends to those who fear him,
>   from generation to generation.
> ⁵¹ He has performed mighty deeds with his arm;
>   he has scattered those who are proud in their inmost thoughts.
> ⁵² He has brought down rulers from their thrones
>   but has lifted up the humble.
> ⁵³ He has filled the hungry with good things
>   but has sent the rich away empty.

> [54] He has helped his servant Israel,
> remembering to be merciful
> [55] to Abraham and his descendants forever,
> just as he promised our ancestors."

[56] Mary stayed with Elizabeth for about three months and then returned home. [57] When it was time for Elizabeth to have her baby, she gave birth to a son. [58] Her neighbors and relatives heard that the Lord had shown her great mercy, and they shared her joy. [59] On the eighth day they came to circumcise the child, and they were going to name him after his father Zechariah, [60] but his mother spoke up and said, "No! He is to be called John." [61] They said to her, "There is no one among your relatives who has that name." [62] Then they made signs to his father, to find out what he would like to name the child. [63] He asked for a writing tablet, and to everyone's astonishment he wrote, "His name is John."

[64] Immediately his mouth was opened and his tongue set free, and he began to speak, praising God. [65] All the neighbors were filled with awe, and throughout the hill country of Judea people were talking about all these things. [66] Everyone who heard this wondered about it, asking, "What then is this child going to be?" For the Lord's hand was with him.

REFLECTION

John began his gospel by going cosmic. Matthew began his gospel with a genealogical record. Mark began his gospel with the message that the time of waiting for the Messiah and his kingdom had been completed. Luke begins his gospel by reassuring his readers that he has taken great care to get the facts straight. Christianity is a religion based *in* history and *on* facts.

The identity of Theophilus is unknown. His name ("friend of God") might be a symbol or a substitute for his true name. He might have been a benefactor who had financially supported Luke as he wrote His Gospel and the book of Acts. He needed to be assured of the truthfulness of what he had been taught and Luke is careful to give him what he needs. We should never think that God expects us to deny or suppress the questions we have about His word or His ways.

Zechariah and Elizabeth were a truly righteous couple. Luke wants to assure us that their childlessness did not come from any overt sin in their lives. Childlessness brought deep pain and often shame into a couple's life, especially for the wife. At her advanced age, Elizabeth would have given up on having a child.

Every Jewish woman aspired to be the mother of the Messiah; in God's plan it was Mary, a young teenager on the other side of the life spectrum from Elizabeth, who was chosen. Notice that her humility and obedience go deeper than Zechariah's: she shows none of his unbelief when spoken to by Gabriel.

Our passage reminds us that God often reveals Himself unexpectedly. Sometimes it is on the far side of our lost dreams.

Sometimes it is when we are about to enter a new chapter in life. It is always when God knows it is best. As you read this devotional give God permission to reveal Himself as He best sees fit. But remember too that whenever or wherever God reveals Himself, He expects His people to respond in trusting, and honest obedience.

CORRELATION

For the Lord is righteous, he loves justice; the upright will see his face.
Psalm 11:7

Even in darkness light dawns for the upright, for those who are gracious and compassionate and righteous. Good will come to those who are generous and lend freely, who conduct their affairs with justice.
Psalm 112:4-5

RECITATION

Our Father in Heaven

Hallowed be Your Name

Your Kingdom come,

Your will be done,
 on earth as it is in Heaven.

Give us today our daily bread.

Forgive us our debts,
 as we also have forgiven our debtors.

And lead us not into temptation,
 but deliver us from the evil one.

Matthew 6:9-13

APPLICATION

What has come to mind, either through the passage or in your reflection that you want to remember?

The Birth of Jesus

Passage: Luke 2:1-40

Meditation: Luke 2:1, 3-21
Pause and Reflect Silently
Highlight Key Phrases
Look to and Lift up Christ

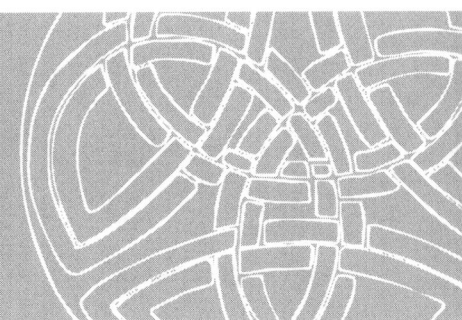

¹*In those days Caesar Augustus issued a decree that a census should be taken of the entire Roman world...* ³*And everyone went to their own town to register.* ⁴*So Joseph also went up from the town of Nazareth in Galilee to Judea, to Bethlehem the town of David, because he belonged to the house and line of David.* ⁵*He went there to register with Mary, who was pledged to be married to him and was expecting a child.*

⁶*While they were there, the time came for the baby to be born,* ⁷*and she gave birth to her firstborn, a son. She wrapped him in cloths and placed him in a manger, because there was no guest room available for them.*

⁸*And there were shepherds living out in the fields nearby, keeping watch over their flocks at night.* ⁹*An angel of the Lord appeared to them, and the glory of the Lord shone around them, and they were terrified.*

¹⁰*But the angel said to them, "Do not be afraid. I bring you*

*good news that will cause great joy for all the people. *[11]*Today in the town of David a Savior has been born to you; he is the Messiah, the Lord. *[12]*This will be a sign to you: You will find a baby wrapped in cloths and lying in a manger."*

[13]*Suddenly a great company of the heavenly host appeared with the angel, praising God and saying,*

[14]*"Glory to God in the highest heaven, and on earth peace to those on whom his favor rests."*

[15]*When the angels had left them and gone into heaven, the shepherds said to one another, "Let's go to Bethlehem and see this thing that has happened, which the Lord has told us about." *[16]*So they hurried off and found Mary and Joseph, and the baby, who was lying in the manger.*

[17]*When they had seen him, they spread the word concerning what had been told them about this child, *[18]*and all who heard it were amazed at what the shepherds said to them. *[19]*But Mary treasured up all these things and pondered them in her heart. *[20]*The shepherds returned, glorifying and praising God for all the things they had heard and seen which were just as they had been told.*

[21]*On the eighth day, when it was time to circumcise the child, he was named Jesus, the name the angel had given him before he was conceived.*

REFLECTION

One can imagine an emotional dark cloud hanging over a Galilean peasant as he traveled to Bethlehem with his betrothed wife at the decree of the Roman emperor. They *had to* be registered and their taxes *had to* be collected. Joseph and Mary were just another poor couple caught up in the grinding oppression of the Roman Empire. Yet their inconvenient journey fulfilled God's divine plan.

Joseph was a direct descendent of David who, through no planning of his own, found himself in the town of David just as his son was to be born. Both he and his wife were aware that they were carrying the future Messiah of Israel. They had little idea what it would actually mean but they had much to be excited and anxious about. As they traveled to Bethlehem, Joseph and Mary might have felt a good deal of relief too: they had probably been hearing the whispers and seeing the looks from people who were not going to believe that God had impregnated an unmarried teenager.

We have no idea how long it was after arriving in Bethlehem that Mary began her labor, but we are more certain today that she gave birth to Jesus in a dirt area within someone's home. It was very common to have an entrance area where the animals were stored in safety at night. There might not have been "room" in the main part of the house but they had a place to lay their heads and a food trough nearby to lay Jesus.

This young family and newborn gave a new dignity to the lives of the poor. The Messiah was not born in a palace surrounded by wealth and privilege but in a plain home that had a difficult future that would be marked by hard labor and simple meals. They did enjoy an unexpected visit from Shepherds one night. Later some magi from the East dropped by. Just the beginning of a life filled with miracles, wonders, suffering and great joy.

CORRELATION

The scepter will not depart from Judah, nor the ruler's staff from between his feet, until he comes to whom it belongs and the obedience of the nations is his.

Genesis 49:10

"But you, Bethlehem Ephrathah, though you are small among the clans of Judah, out of you will come for me one who will be ruler over Israel, whose origins are from of old, from ancient times."

Micah 5:2

RECITATION

Lord Jesus Christ, Son of God, have mercy on me, a sinner.

The Jesus Prayer[10]

>Recite three times slowly.

APPLICATION

What has come to mind, either through the passage or in your reflection that you want to remember?

John The Baptist

Passage: Luke 3:1-20

Meditation: Luke 3:1-20
Pause and Reflect Silently
Highlight Key Phrases
Look to and Lift up Christ

¹*In the fifteenth year of the reign of Tiberius Caesar—when Pontius Pilate was governor of Judea, Herod tetrarch of Galilee, his brother Philip tetrarch of Iturea and Traconitis, and Lysanias tetrarch of Abilene— ²during the high-priesthood of Annas and Caiaphas, the word of God came to John son of Zechariah in the wilderness. ³He went into all the country around the Jordan, preaching a baptism of repentance for the forgiveness of sins. ⁴As it is written in the book of the words of Isaiah the prophet:*

> *"A voice of one calling in the wilderness,*
> *'Prepare the way for the Lord,*
>   *make straight paths for him.*
> *⁵Every valley shall be filled in,*
>   *every mountain and hill made low.*
> *The crooked roads shall become straight,*
>   *the rough ways smooth.*
> *⁶And all people will see God's salvation.'"*

⁷John said to the crowds coming out to be baptized by him, "You brood of vipers! Who warned you to flee from the coming wrath? ⁸Produce fruit in keeping with repentance. And do not begin to say to yourselves, 'We have Abraham as our father.' For I tell you that out of these stones God can raise up children for Abraham. ⁹The ax is already at the root of the trees, and every tree that does not produce good fruit will be cut down and thrown into the fire."

¹⁰"What should we do then?" the crowd asked. ¹¹John answered, "Anyone who has two shirts should share with the one who has none, and anyone who has food should do the same." ¹²Even tax collectors came to be baptized. "Teacher," they asked, "what should we do?" ¹³"Don't collect any more than you are required to," he told them. ¹⁴Then some soldiers asked him, "And what should we do?" He replied, "Don't extort money and don't accuse people falsely—be content with your pay."

¹⁵The people were waiting expectantly and were all wondering in their hearts if John might possibly be the Messiah. ¹⁶John answered them all, "I baptize you with water. But one who is more powerful than I will come, the straps of whose sandals I am not worthy to untie. He will baptize you with the Holy Spirit and fire. ¹⁷His winnowing fork is in his hand to clear his threshing floor and to gather the wheat into his barn, but he will burn up the chaff with unquenchable fire." ¹⁸And with many other words John exhorted the people and proclaimed the good news to them.

¹⁹But when John rebuked Herod the tetrarch because of his marriage to Herodias, his brother's wife, and all the other evil things he had done, ²⁰Herod added this to them all: He locked John up in prison.

REFLECTION

If Caesar Tiberius' reign is dated from Caesar Augustus' death (A.D. 14), his "fifteenth year" would have been from August A.D. 28 to August A.D. 29. That would mean that John the Baptist's ministry began around A.D. 28.

John pulled no punches in his messages to the people. Like Jesus later, he was willing to tell it like it is. Calling the religious leaders a "brood of vipers" did not endear him to the power brokers of his time but it did send a message to the people that he treated everyone equally in their need for God.

John was famous in his own right but his lasting contribution was that he prepared people to hear Jesus' message. In the last book of the Old Testament, Malachi prophesied that one would come in the spirit of Elijah to prepare the people for their Messiah. Malachi said, "Then suddenly the Lord you are seeking will come to his temple; the messenger of the covenant, whom you desire, will come," says the Lord Almighty. But who can endure the day of his coming? Who can stand when he appears, for he will be like a refiner's fire? (3:1-2a)."

To be able to stand before the Messiah who they so longed to see, the people would need to be painfully honest with themselves and God about their sin. It would take deep "heart surgery" but it was essential if they were going to be able to personally benefit from his coming. Why? Sin produces resistance and resentment toward God; it develops calluses on our hearts and "scales" over our eyes. Those who did not take care of their sin problem reacted hostilely to Jesus when he came. Those who came forward to be baptized by John publically admitted that they were sinners in need of God's cleansing. Their admission and submission gave them a fresh start and a soft heart. They were the ones who largely turned to Christ. Jesus would have been like a fresh breeze and "manna" from heaven to them.

CORRELATION

They came to John and said to him, "Rabbi, that man who was with you on the other side of the Jordan—the one you testified about—look, he is baptizing, and everyone is going to him." To this John replied, "A person can receive only what is given them from heaven. You yourselves can testify that I said, 'I am not the Messiah but am sent ahead of him.'...
The friend who attends the bridegroom waits and listens for him, and is full of joy when he hears the bridegroom's voice. That joy is mine, and it is now complete. He must become greater; I must become less."

John 3:26-28, 29b-30

RECITATION

I believe in God the Father, Almighty Maker of heaven and earth.

And in Jesus Christ his only Son our Lord; who was conceived by the Holy Spirit, born of the Virgin Mary, suffered under Pontius Pilate, was crucified, dead, and buried; he descended into hell; the third day he rose again from the dead;

He ascended into heaven, and sits on the right hand of God the Father Almighty; from there he shall come to judge the living and the dead.

I believe in the Holy Spirit; the holy Christian Church; the communion of saints; the forgiveness of sins; the resurrection of the body; and the life everlasting. AMEN.[11]

The Apostle's Creed

APPLICATION

What has come to mind, either through the passage or in your reflection that you want to remember?

Jesus' Baptism and Temptation

Passage: Matthew 3:13-4:17

Meditation: Matthew 3:13-4:17
Pause and Reflect Silently
Highlight Key Phrases
Look to and Lift up Christ

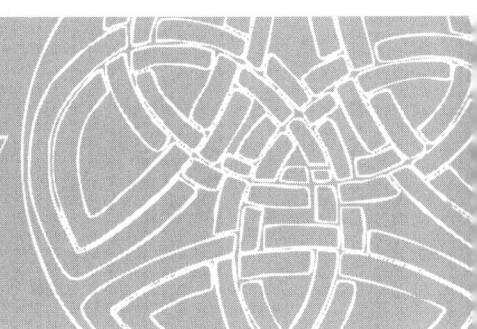

¹³Then Jesus came from Galilee to the Jordan to be baptized by John. ¹⁴But John tried to deter him, saying, "I need to be baptized by you, and do you come to me?" ¹⁵Jesus replied, "Let it be so now; it is proper for us to do this to fulfill all righteousness." Then John consented.

¹⁶As soon as Jesus was baptized, he went up out of the water. At that moment heaven was opened, and he saw the Spirit of God descending like a dove and alighting on him. ¹⁷And a voice from heaven said, "This is my Son, whom I love; with him I am well pleased."

4¹Then Jesus was led by the Spirit into the wilderness to be tempted by the devil. ²After fasting forty days and forty nights, he was hungry.

³The tempter came to him and said, "If you are the Son of God, tell these stones to become bread." ⁴Jesus answered, "It is written:

'Man shall not live on bread alone, but on every word that comes from the mouth of God.'"

⁵Then the devil took him to the holy city and had him stand on the highest point of the temple. ⁶"If you are the Son of God," he said, "throw yourself down. For it is written: '"He will command his angels concerning you, and they will lift you up in their hands, so that you will not strike your foot against a stone.'" ⁷Jesus answered him, "It is also written: 'Do not put the Lord your God to the test.'"

⁸Again, the devil took him to a very high mountain and showed him all the kingdoms of the world and their splendor. ⁹"All this I will give you," he said, "if you will bow down and worship me."

¹⁰Jesus said to him, "Away from me, Satan! For it is written: 'Worship the Lord your God, and serve him only.'" ¹¹Then the devil left him, and angels came and attended him.

¹²When Jesus heard that John had been put in prison, he withdrew to Galilee. ¹³Leaving Nazareth, he went and lived in Capernaum, which was by the lake in the area of Zebulun and Naphtali—¹⁴to fulfill what was said through the prophet Isaiah: ¹⁵"Land of Zebulun and land of Naphtali, the Way of the Sea, beyond the Jordan, Galilee of the Gentiles—¹⁶the people living in darkness have seen a great light; on those living in the land of the shadow of death a light has dawned."

¹⁷From that time on Jesus began to preach, "Repent, for the kingdom of heaven has come near."

REFLECTION

From the moment he was born, Jesus identified with us in our humanity and fallen condition. Though he was sinless in his conception and throughout his life, Jesus still had to learn to submit to, trust in and obey His Father. He had done so perfectly but privately up to that moment when John baptized him.

God's word of affirmation to Jesus reflects Isaiah 42:1 ("Here is my servant, whom I uphold, my chosen one in whom I delight; I will put my Spirit upon him") and Psalm 2:7 ("You are my Son.") Before Jesus had done anything spectacular or been noticed by the public, he had lived a life that had well-pleased His Father. As Heaven itself opened and the Spirit of God descended on him as a dove, Jesus stood in the water beside John, showing publically that he had come to do His Father's will and to identify with mankind in their sin and need for God.

As we read about his baptism we should remind ourselves that it was the dawning of a new era: the transition had begun from the Old Covenant era in which God's people lived under the Law given to Moses into the New Covenant era in which God's people would now live under Christ and in the power of his Spirit (the very One who empowered *his* life and resurrection).

As we read about his temptation, we should remind ourselves that Jesus did not take the easy road to achieve our salvation: he faced the full force of satanic temptation as a man and did not turn to his divine attributes for help.

We see much to reflect on in the temptations. Let's reflect on two.

First, Jesus chose to live in complete dependence on God. If there was anyone who could have lived a self-sufficient, rock-star famous, militarily powerful life, it was him. Yet he knew that he had not been called to that life. *Second*, Jesus defeated Satan because He had fully internalized and treasured God's word. He is the epitome of everything God intended for us to be! He is Good News in every sense.

CORRELATION

During the days of Jesus' life on earth, he offered up prayers and petitions with loud cries and tears to the one who could save him from death, and he was heard because of his reverent submission. Although he was a son, he learned obedience from what he suffered and, once made perfect, he became the source of eternal salvation for all who obey him... Hebrews 5:7-9

RECITATION

O Father, light up
  the small duties of this day's life;

May they shine
  with the beauty of Your countenance.

May we believe that glory can dwell
  in the commonest task of every day.

Augustine of Hippo[12]

APPLICATION

What has come to mind, either through the passage or in your reflection that you want to remember?

The Sermon On The Mount, Part 1

Passage: Matthew 5:1-48

Meditation: Matthew 5:2-20
Pause and Reflect Silently
Highlight Key Phrases
Look to and Lift up Christ

His disciples came to him, ²and he began to teach them. He said:

³"Blessed are the poor in spirit,
  for theirs is the kingdom of heaven.
⁴Blessed are those who mourn,
  for they will be comforted.
⁵Blessed are the meek,
  for they will inherit the earth.
⁶Blessed are those who hunger and thirst for righteousness,
  for they will be filled.
⁷Blessed are the merciful,
  for they will be shown mercy.
⁸Blessed are the pure in heart,
  for they will see God.
⁹Blessed are the peacemakers,
  for they will be called children of God.
¹⁰Blessed are those who are persecuted because of righteousness,
  for theirs is the kingdom of heaven.

¹¹*Blessed are you when people insult you, persecute you and falsely say all kinds of evil against you because of me.*

¹²*Rejoice and be glad, because great is your reward in heaven, for in the same way they persecuted the prophets who were before you.*

¹³*You are the salt of the earth. But if the salt loses its saltiness, how can it be made salty again? It is no longer good for anything, except to be thrown out and trampled underfoot.* ¹⁴*You are the light of the world. A town built on a hill cannot be hidden.* ¹⁵*Neither do people light a lamp and put it under a bowl. Instead they put it on its stand, and it gives light to everyone in the house.* ¹⁶*In the same way, let your light shine before others, that they may see your good deeds and glorify your Father in heaven.*

¹⁷*Do not think that I have come to abolish the Law or the Prophets; I have not come to abolish them but to fulfill them.* ¹⁸*For truly I tell you, until heaven and earth disappear, not the smallest letter, not the least stroke of a pen, will by any means disappear from the Law until everything is accomplished.* ¹⁹*Therefore anyone who sets aside one of the least of these commands and teaches others accordingly will be called least in the kingdom of heaven, but whoever practices and teaches these commands will be called great in the kingdom of heaven.* ²⁰*For I tell you that unless your righteousness surpasses that of the Pharisees and the teachers of the law, you will certainly not enter the kingdom of heaven.*

REFLECTION

The Sermon on the Mount is a simplified account of Jesus' teaching on living a righteous life. At this point, Jesus had not yet chosen his twelve apostles and had a growing number of people turning to him.

In the ancient world people followed great teachers to be mentored in how to live life: such followers were called disciples. This Sermon is Jesus' blueprint on how he makes disciples. It shows how he develops *his* mind, motives and ministry in his followers' lives. Notice that he is less concerned about managing behavior and more concerned about helping his disciples develop minds and hearts that are formed by and filled with a hunger for God's righteousness, or inner goodness. It is only such a person that can live the godly life that Jesus embodied and thus go beyond the practices of the religious and philosophical schools of his (and our) time.

Jesus begins with the Beatitudes; talks about his disciples' relationships with the world and the Law given to Moses and then deals with the sin issues of the heart. The Beatitudes, in their "blessed are they who" form, should shock us in what they say about the truly blessed life. It is not a life of ease, popularity and earthly success: it is a life of dependence on God and inner transformation that leads us to become people who are marked by inner purity and relational peace-making.

Jesus had already begun sharing the good news that the Kingdom of God was now available before he presented this sermon. There are a number of different opinions on how to understand the Kingdom of God. We will talk about them more when we read Matthew 13.

Here we will mention the wonderful truth that God's restoration power is available to us now. When we turn to Christ all of His heavenly resources become available to us. The Sermon then is Jesus' teaching on how to access His heavenly treasures so that we can live *like* him and *for* him in every area of our life.

CORRELATION

Righteousness and justice are the foundation of your throne; love and faithfulness go before you. Blessed are those who have learned to acclaim you, who walk in the light of your presence, Lord. They rejoice in your name all day long; they celebrate your righteousness. Psalm 89:14-16

RECITATION

LORD, MAKE ME AN INSTRUMENT OF YOUR PEACE,

where there is hatred, let me sow love,

where there is injury, pardon,

where there is discord, may I bring harmony,

where there is error, may I bring truth,

where there is doubt, may I bring faith,

where there is despair, may I bring hope,

where there is darkness, may I bring light,

and where there is sadness, may I bring joy.

O Divine Master,

grant that I may not so much seek

To be consoled, as to console,

to be understood, as to understand,

to be loved, as to love.

for it is in giving that we receive;

it is in pardoning that we are pardoned;

and it is in dying that we are born into eternal life.

Francis of Assisi

APPLICATION

What has come to mind, either through the passage or in your reflection that you want to remember?

The Sermon On The Mount, Part 2

Passage: Matthew 6:1-7:29

Meditation: Matthew 7:1-23
Pause and Reflect Silently
Highlight Key Phrases
Look to and Lift up Christ

Do not judge, or you too will be judged. ²For in the same way you judge others, you will be judged, and with the measure you use, it will be measured to you. ³Why do you look at the speck of sawdust in your brother's eye and pay no attention to the plank in your own eye? ⁴How can you say to your brother, 'Let me take the speck out of your eye,' when all the time there is a plank in your own eye? ⁵You hypocrite, first take the plank out of your own eye, and then you will see clearly to remove the speck from your brother's eye.

⁶Do not give dogs what is sacred; do not throw your pearls to pigs. If you do, they may trample them under their feet, and turn and tear you to pieces.

⁷Ask and it will be given to you; seek and you will find; knock and the door will be opened to you. ⁸For everyone who asks receives; the one who seeks finds; and to the one who knocks, the door will be opened.

⁹Which of you, if your son asks for bread, will give him a stone? ¹⁰Or if he asks for a fish, will give him a snake? ¹¹If you, then, though you are evil, know how to give good gifts to your children, how much more will your Father in heaven give good gifts to those who ask him! ¹²So in everything, do to others what you would have them do to you, for this sums up the Law and the Prophets.

¹³Enter through the narrow gate. For wide is the gate and broad is the road that leads to destruction, and many enter through it. ¹⁴But small is the gate and narrow the road that leads to life, and only a few find it

¹⁵Watch out for false prophets. They come to you in sheep's clothing, but inwardly they are ferocious wolves. ¹⁶By their fruit you will recognize them. Do people pick grapes from thornbushes, or figs from thistles? ¹⁷Likewise, every good tree bears good fruit, but a bad tree bears bad fruit. ¹⁸A good tree cannot bear bad fruit, and a bad tree cannot bear good fruit. ¹⁹Every tree that does not bear good fruit is cut down and thrown into the fire. ²⁰Thus, by their fruit you will recognize them.

²¹Not everyone who says to me, 'Lord, Lord,' will enter the kingdom of heaven, but only the one who does the will of my Father who is in heaven. ²²Many will say to me on that day, 'Lord, Lord, did we not prophesy in your name and in your name drive out demons and in your name perform many miracles?' ²³Then I will tell them plainly, 'I never knew you. Away from me, you evildoers!'

REFLECTION

In the second half of the Sermon, Jesus turns his attention to true worship and wisdom. Rick Warren began his best-selling book, *The Purpose-Driven Life*, with a simple but profound statement: "**It's not about you.**"[13] As you apply the Sermon in your life keep this statement in mind.

To fully develop the heart of goodness that Jesus intends for us we need to keep his individual sayings in their original context. We can benefit from practicing the Lord's Prayer or applying his insights on worry, but to experience his full intention we need to ask how well we are doing with what he has said *before* these passages. Are we seeing our life experiences the way Jesus sees them (The Beatitudes)? Are we relating to the world and to the Mosaic Law the way Jesus taught (Salt & Light)? Are we doing the hard work of cleansing the inside of our hearts? These are what make it possible for us to develop a life of genuine worship and wisdom.

If we use the Sermon as a pathway for spiritual training it will come alive and play the role Jesus intended for it to have. Only then will Giving, Praying, Fasting, and Seeking God lead to true and lasting life change and not religious pride. It is not enough to agree to a set of beliefs, or to try harder to live a godly life: we need to learn to see the way Jesus sees and do the things that Jesus said we should do.

As we emulate Jesus' way we will face many situations in which we do not know the answers. Jesus does not give us answers to every situation. He gives us principles and stories to take with us so that we can learn to discern the best way to face what comes our way.

Throughout the Sermon there is another element that is easy to miss: we are meant to live in community with other disciples. We were never meant to live the Christian life alone. As we apply the insights of the Sermon to our lives it is essential that we do so with other growing Christians!

CORRELATION

And now, Israel, what does the Lord your God ask of you but to fear the Lord your God, to walk in obedience to him, to love him, to serve the Lord your God with all your heart and with all your soul, and to observe the Lord's commands and decrees that I am giving you today for your own good?
Deuteronomy 10:12-13

RECITATION

Thanks be to you, our Lord Jesus Christ,

For all the benefits you have given us,

For all the pains and insults you have borne for us.

Most merciful Redeemer, Friend, and Brother,

May we know you more clearly,

Love you more dearly,

And follow you more nearly:

Forever and ever. AMEN.

Richard Chichester[14]

APPLICATION

What has come to mind, either through the passage or in your reflection that you want to remember?

The Kingdom of Heaven

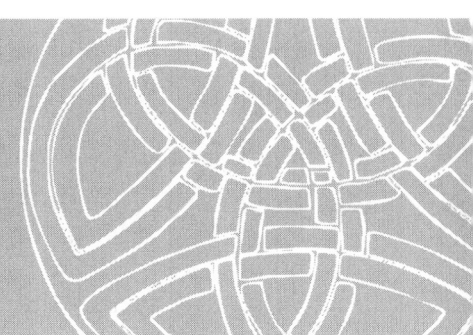

Passage: Matthew 13:1-45

Meditation: Matthew 13:18-33
Pause and Reflect Silently
Highlight Key Phrases
Look to and Lift up Christ

[18]"Listen then to what the parable of the sower means: [19]When anyone hears the message about the kingdom and does not understand it, the evil one comes and snatches away what was sown in their heart. This is the seed sown along the path.

[20]The seed falling on rocky ground refers to someone who hears the word and at once receives it with joy. [21]But since they have no root, they last only a short time. When trouble or persecution comes because of the word, they quickly fall away.

[22]The seed falling among the thorns refers to someone who hears the word, but the worries of this life and the deceitfulness of wealth choke the word, making it unfruitful.

[23]But the seed falling on good soil refers to someone who hears the word and understands it. This is the one who produces a crop, yielding a hundred, sixty or thirty times what was sown."

[24]Jesus told them another parable: "The kingdom of heaven is

like a man who sowed good seed in his field. ²⁵But while everyone was sleeping, his enemy came and sowed weeds among the wheat, and went away. ²⁶When the wheat sprouted and formed heads, then the weeds also appeared.

²⁷"The owner's servants came to him and said, 'Sir, didn't you sow good seed in your field? Where then did the weeds come from?' ²⁸"'An enemy did this,' he replied. "The servants asked him, 'Do you want us to go and pull them up?'

²⁹"'No,' he answered, 'because while you are pulling the weeds, you may uproot the wheat with them. ³⁰Let both grow together until the harvest. At that time I will tell the harvesters: First collect the weeds and tie them in bundles to be burned; then gather the wheat and bring it into my barn.'"

³¹He told them another parable: "The kingdom of heaven is like a mustard seed, which a man took and planted in his field. ³²Though it is the smallest of all seeds, yet when it grows, it is the largest of garden plants and becomes a tree, so that the birds come and perch in its branches."

³³He told them still another parable: "The kingdom of heaven is like yeast that a woman took and mixed into about sixty pounds of flour until it worked all through the dough."

REFLECTION

There are a number of perspectives on the Kingdom of God. By the first century, during Jesus' lifetime, the Jewish people had come to expect the Kingdom to be a military-political empire led by their Messiah. They believed it would dominate the world powers around them. Jesus' message confused the Jewish people because his teachings had nothing to do with dominating or destroying their enemies. Jesus frustrated people further by using stories from everyday life that they had never connected with the Kingdom of God.

The central concept behind the Kingdom is the idea of *rulership*: the reign of God, specially advanced through the Jewish Messiah. As people study Jesus' teachings some conclude that the Kingdom is a future reign that will begin when Jesus returns. Others see the Kingdom as a present reign that is at work in people's lives today. Ask yourself this: when you pray, "Your kingdom come," are you asking God to hurry the Second Coming or asking Him to do something in your present situation? Many believe that the Kingdom includes both present and future facets. The Kingdom is available to us "now"; yet our access to it is just a foretaste of its full transformative power, which has "not yet" been manifested.

In this passage, Jesus focuses on how the Kingdom works in our present world. He uses activities like sowing seeds, pulling weeds and catching fish to reveal how God's rule works and relates to the fallen realities of our present age. It is not a "coercive" power that grows through a military army but a "small," seemingly insignificant, power that grows through a message (The Gospel). But though it starts small, it will one day spread throughout the earth.

The passage peaks with the parables of the Pearl and Hidden Treasure. They teach that Jesus' present kingdom goal is to bring his disciples to a place where they willingly and joyfully give up everything they have and everything they are to God because of their discovery of the full riches they have found in His Kingdom.

CORRELATION

"If I drive out demons by the Spirit of God, then the kingdom of God has come upon you."
~Jesus   Matthew 12:28

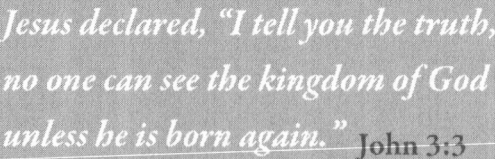

Jesus declared, "I tell you the truth, no one can see the kingdom of God unless he is born again." John 3:3

RECITATION

Lord, whatever this day may bring

Your name be praised.

Be gracious to me and help me.

Grant me strength to bear whatever you may send,
  and let not fear overrule me.

I trust your grace and commit my life wholly into your
  hands.

Whether I live or whether I die, I am with you.

And you are with me,

O my Lord and my God.

Lord, I wait for your salvation,
  and for the coming of your kingdom. AMEN.[15]

Dietrich Bonhoeffer

APPLICATION

What has come to mind, either through the passage or in your reflection that you want to remember?

The Good Samaritan

Passage: Luke 10:25-37

Meditation: Luke 10:25-37
Pause and Reflect Silently
Highlight Key Phrases
Look to and Lift up Christ

²⁵*On one occasion an expert in the law stood up to test Jesus. "Teacher," he asked, "what must I do to inherit eternal life?"*

²⁶*"What is written in the Law?" he replied. "How do you read it?"*

²⁷*He answered, "'Love the Lord your God with all your heart and with all your soul and with all your strength and with all your mind'; and, 'Love your neighbor as yourself.'"*

²⁸*"You have answered correctly," Jesus replied. "Do this and you will live."*

²⁹*But he wanted to justify himself, so he asked Jesus, "And who is my neighbor?"*

³⁰*In reply Jesus said: "A man was going down from Jerusalem to Jericho, when he was attacked by robbers. They stripped him of his clothes, beat him and went away, leaving him half dead.*

³¹A priest happened to be going down the same road, and when he saw the man, he passed by on the other side. ³²So too, a Levite, when he came to the place and saw him, passed by on the other side.

³³But a Samaritan, as he traveled, came where the man was; and when he saw him, he took pity on him. ³⁴He went to him and bandaged his wounds, pouring on oil and wine. Then he put the man on his own donkey, brought him to an inn and took care of him. ³⁵The next day he took out two denarii and gave them to the innkeeper. 'Look after him,' he said, 'and when I return, I will reimburse you for any extra expense you may have.'

³⁶"Which of these three do you think was a neighbor to the man who fell into the hands of robbers?"

³⁷The expert in the law replied, "The one who had mercy on him."

Jesus told him, "Go and do likewise."

REFLECTION

Our world has come a long way from the universal brutality of the ancient world but it still has so far to go! You likely have someone in your life that is consistently frustrating. And there is probably someone you so dislike that you can't think of or wish for anything good for them. Such are the realities of our daily lives.

Be encouraged by the fact that Jesus' teachings have done more to change the world than any other religious or military figure in history. Yet his stories can become so familiar that they lose their ability to shock us enough to change the way we look at our lives and relationships.

Samaritans were hated half-breeds to the Jewish people. The Jewish people felt justified in their contempt for them and believed that God agreed with their attitudes. Their origin went back to 722 BC when a small remnant of Northern Israelites began inter-marrying with non-Jews who had come from other regions of the Assyrian Empire (after it had destroyed the Northern Kingdom of Israel).

They accepted only the first five books of Moses (Pentateuch) and rejected the rest of the Old Testament. They replaced true worship with their own idolatrous worship. In 128 BC the Jewish leader John Hyrcanus burned the Samaritan's temple down. The Samaritans had returned the hatred with their own and the two peoples had spent centuries despising and avoiding each other. Jesus' use of a Samaritan as a role model would have given his followers a sickening feeling and surfaced serious hostility.

Today, let's rejoice that Jesus rejected ethnic hatred and accepted people regardless of their backgrounds. We know this is the way things should be. But as we see how unloving the priest and Levite were, let us look to our own hearts first. We need to accept that there is a very thin line between dislike and hatred. Present any frustration and hostility you might have towards others to God, and ask Him to heal what is beyond our human ability to fix.

CORRELATION

If your enemy is hungry, feed him; if he is thirsty, give him something to drink. In doing this, you will heap burning coals on his head." Do not be overcome by evil, but overcome evil with good.

Romans 12:20-21

RECITATION

GOD, GRANT ME THE SERENITY
 to accept the things I cannot change;

Courage to change the things I can and
 the wisdom to know the difference.

To live one day at a time;
 enjoying one moment at a time;

Accepting hardship as the pathway to peace.

To take, as He did, this sinful world as it is, not as I would
 have it.

Trusting that He will make all things right if I surrender to
 His Will.

That I may be reasonably happy in this life and supremely
 happy with You forever in the next. AMEN.

Reinhold Neibuhr

APPLICATION

What has come to mind, either through the passage or in your reflection that you want to remember?

Lost and Found

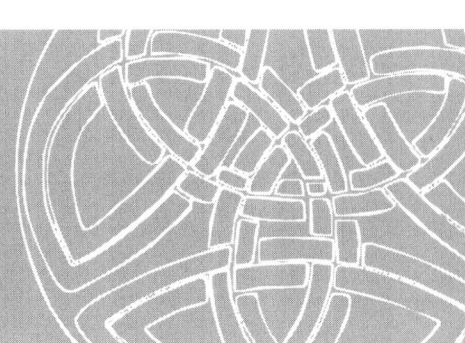

Passage: Luke 15:1-32

Meditation: Luke 15: 17-32
Pause and Reflect Silently
Highlight Key Phrases
Look to and Lift up Christ

[17] "When [the younger brother] came to his senses, he said, 'How many of my father's hired servants have food to spare, and here I am starving to death!

[18] I will set out and go back to my father and say to him: Father, I have sinned against heaven and against you. [19] I am no longer worthy to be called your son; make me like one of your hired servants.' [20] So he got up and went to his father.

"But while he was still a long way off, his father saw him and was filled with compassion for him; he ran to his son, threw his arms around him and kissed him.

[21] "The son said to him, 'Father, I have sinned against heaven and against you. I am no longer worthy to be called your son.'

[22] "But the father said to his servants, 'Quick! Bring the best robe and put it on him. Put a ring on his finger and sandals on his feet. [23] Bring the fattened calf and kill it. Let's have a feast and

celebrate. ²⁴For this son of mine was dead and is alive again; he was lost and is found.' So they began to celebrate.

²⁵"Meanwhile, the older son was in the field. When he came near the house, he heard music and dancing. ²⁶So he called one of the servants and asked him what was going on. ²⁷'Your brother has come,' he replied, 'and your father has killed the fattened calf because he has him back safe and sound.'

²⁸"The older brother became angry and refused to go in. So his father went out and pleaded with him. ²⁹But he answered his father, 'Look! All these years I've been slaving for you and never disobeyed your orders. Yet you never gave me even a young goat so I could celebrate with my friends. ³⁰But when this son of yours who has squandered your property with prostitutes comes home, you kill the fattened calf for him!'

³¹"'My son,' the father said, 'you are always with me, and everything I have is yours. ³²But we had to celebrate and be glad, because this brother of yours was dead and is alive again; he was lost and is found.'"

REFLECTION

The story of the prodigal son is one of Jesus' most well-loved. If you were asked to show how the Christian view of God differs from other religions this is the passage to turn to. There is no image of God like this in Islam, Hinduism or any other religious system.

Jesus uses the stories of a shepherd and a widow to set the stage. The shepherd is concerned for one sheep among a hundred, while the widow is concerned for one coin among ten: wouldn't a truly loving father be concerned for one son among two?

Jesus' picture of a father's gracious love for his sinning son moves us towards a bigger and more wonderful picture of our heavenly Father. Notice that the father ran toward his son. Jewish men had to bunch their long robes together at their waists to run and it was a very undignified looking spectacle. But other's expectations meant nothing to this father when it came to welcoming his returning son. Our heavenly Father could not care less for people's social sensibilities when it comes to embracing his returning children, *regardless of where they have come from*!

The religious leaders wondered, "Didn't Jesus realize that accepting and loving people like that *before* they had cleaned up their lives would just make the problem worse?" Jesus was attracting people who were morally and ethically broken. He warmly welcomed tax collectors who were oppressing the people. He healed and loved "sinners" who had disregarded the Mosaic Law and the traditions of their elders. Wasn't Jesus encouraging people to sin and disregard God? Such were the thoughts of the religious leaders of his time, and such are the thoughts of *religious* thinkers in all times! Their attitude is captured in the older son's inability to enter into his father's joy at the return of his erring son; it kept him, and all religious people, from getting what Jesus is all about and how he changes lives.

CORRELATION

*The **LORD**, the **LORD**, a compassionate and gracious God, slow to anger, abounding in love and faithfulness, maintaining love to thousands and forgiving wickedness, rebellion and sin. Yet He does not leave the guilty unpunished.*

Exodus 34:6-7

Jesus straightened up and asked her, "Woman, where are they? Has no one condemned you?" "No one, sir," she said. "Then neither do I condemn you," Jesus declared. "Go now and leave your life of sin."

John 8:10-11

RECITATION

Father, we give you thanks for all the gifts you freely bestow on us. For the beauty and wonder of your creation, in earth and sky and sea, Lord, we thank you.

For our daily food and drink, our homes and families, and our friends, Lord, we thank you.

For minds to think, and hearts to love, and hands to serve, Lord, we thank you. For health and strength to work, and leisure to rest and play, Lord, we thank you.

For the brave and courageous, who are patient in suffering and faithful in adversity, Lord, we thank you.

For the communion of saints, in all times and places, Lord, we thank you.

Above all, we give you thanks for the great mercies and promises given to us in Christ Jesus our Lord; to him be praise and glory, with you, O Father, and the Holy Spirit, now and forever. AMEN.[16]

APPLICATION

What has come to mind, either through the passage or in your reflection that you want to remember?

Feeding The Five Thousand

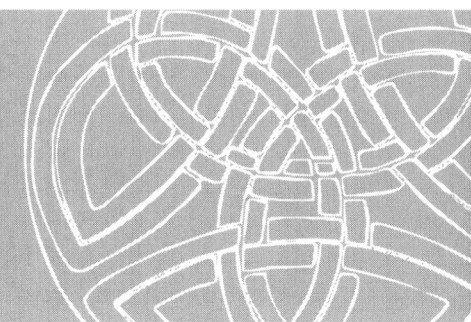

Passage: Luke 9:1-27

Meditation: Luke 9: 1-17
Pause and Reflect Silently
Highlight Key Phrases
Look to and Lift up Christ

¹*When Jesus had called the Twelve together, he gave them power and authority to drive out all demons and to cure diseases, ²and he sent them out to proclaim the kingdom of God and to heal the sick.*

³*He told them: "Take nothing for the journey—no staff, no bag, no bread, no money, no extra shirt. ⁴Whatever house you enter, stay there until you leave that town. ⁵If people do not welcome you, leave their town and shake the dust off your feet as a testimony against them." ⁶So they set out and went from village to village, proclaiming the good news and healing people everywhere.*

⁷*Now Herod the tetrarch heard about all that was going on. And he was perplexed because some were saying that John had been raised from the dead, ⁸others that Elijah had appeared, and still others that one of the prophets of long ago had come back to life. ⁹But Herod said, "I beheaded John. Who, then, is this I hear such things about?" And he tried to see him.*

¹⁰When the apostles returned, they reported to Jesus what they had done. Then he took them with him and they withdrew by themselves to a town called Bethsaida, ¹¹but the crowds learned about it and followed him. He welcomed them and spoke to them about the kingdom of God, and healed those who needed healing.

¹²Late in the afternoon the Twelve came to him and said, "Send the crowd away so they can go to the surrounding villages and countryside and find food and lodging, because we are in a remote place here." ¹³He replied, "You give them something to eat."

They answered, "We have only five loaves of bread and two fish—unless we go and buy food for all this crowd." ¹⁴(About five thousand men were there.)

But he said to his disciples, "Have them sit down in groups of about fifty each." ¹⁵The disciples did so, and everyone sat down. ¹⁶Taking the five loaves and the two fish and looking up to heaven, he gave thanks and broke them. Then he gave them to the disciples to distribute to the people. ¹⁷They all ate and were satisfied, and the disciples picked up twelve basketfuls of broken pieces that were left over.

REFLECTION

The Apostles had just returned from a ministry trip. Jesus had sent them out but had not gone with them. They had experienced the joy and awe of seeing God free and heal people through them. Ministry depletes you, though, and they likely came back exhausted and grateful just to be with Jesus again.

Jesus seems to have immediately left town with them but the crowds had followed. Thus, a planned retreat became another long day of ministry. Jesus welcomed everyone, healed those who had need, and taught them. As the day ended, the disciples realized that the people would need to eat and that they were in an isolated area. Even though the disciples were bone tired and had nothing to offer, Jesus pressured them to find a solution. The disciples had nothing. They could only scare up a little bread and fish from a young boy.

Think how frustrating the situation must have been. Their retreat had been lost. Their Rabbi had been busy all day helping others. Neither the crowd *nor they themselves* had come prepared. Now they were heading toward a crisis and all they had were five loaves of bread and two fish. But they did what Jesus told them to do and presented what little they had to him. Notice that Jesus did not put pressure on them to force them to fix the problem: they couldn't. Jesus put pressure on them so that they would turn to Him to take care of the situation.

Jesus might have prayed a Jewish prayer from the time: "Blessed are You, O Lord our God, King of the Universe, who brings forth bread from the earth." He then broke the bread and tore the fish and *regenerated* new bread and fish as he went. It's not mentioned how many understood what was happening but the disciples were first-hand witnesses and participants in the miracle. Every time they returned to Jesus they had a fresh supply of fish and a reminder of his miraculous power!

CORRELATION

Then Jesus declared, "I am the bread of life. He who comes to me will never go hungry, and he who believes in me will never be thirsty.
John 6:35

When Moses' hands grew tired, they took a stone and put it under him and he sat on it. Aaron and Hur held his hands up—one on one side, one on the other—so that his hands remained steady till sunset.
Exodus 17:12

RECITATION

Lord, you have been our dwelling place throughout all generations.

Before the mountains were born or you brought forth the universe, from everlasting to everlasting, you are God.

Forgive us our sins that we might not be consumed by your anger.

Teach us to number our days that we may gain a heart of wisdom.

Satisfy us in the morning with your unfailing love, that we may sing for joy and be glad in all our days.

Heal us and restore us from our afflictions, Lord, for this world is filled with many troubles.

May your favor rest upon us, and may the work of our hands be established by You, Father.

A prayer based on Psalm 90

APPLICATION

What has come to mind, either through the passage or in your reflection that you want to remember?

Walking On Water

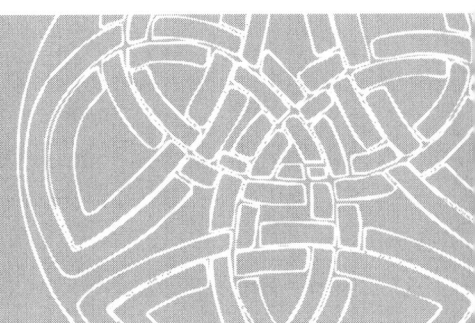

Passage: Matthew 14:22-36

Meditation: Matthew 14:22-36
Pause and Reflect Silently
Highlight Key Phrases
Look to and Lift up Christ

²²*Immediately Jesus made the disciples get into the boat and go on ahead of him to the other side, while he dismissed the crowd.*

²³*After he had dismissed them, he went up on a mountainside by himself to pray. Later that night, he was there alone,* ²⁴*and the boat was already a considerable distance from land, buffeted by the waves because the wind was against it.*

²⁵*Shortly before dawn Jesus went out to them, walking on the lake.* ²⁶*When the disciples saw him walking on the lake, they were terrified. "It's a ghost," they said, and cried out in fear.*

²⁷*But Jesus immediately said to them: "Take courage! It is I. Don't be afraid."*

²⁸*"Lord, if it's you," Peter replied, "tell me to come to you on the water."*

²⁹*"Come," he said.*

Then Peter got down out of the boat, walked on the water and came toward Jesus. ³⁰But when he saw the wind, he was afraid and, beginning to sink, cried out, "Lord, save me!"

³¹Immediately Jesus reached out his hand and caught him. "You of little faith," he said, "why did you doubt?"

³²And when they climbed into the boat, the wind died down. ³³Then those who were in the boat worshiped him, saying, "Truly you are the Son of God."

³⁴When they had crossed over, they landed at Gennesaret. ³⁵And when the men of that place recognized Jesus, they sent word to all the surrounding country. People brought all their sick to him ³⁶and begged him to let the sick just touch the edge of his cloak, and all who touched it were healed.

REFLECTION

One of the most frightening moments in the disciples' lives turned out to be one of the most significant.

Dallas Willard, in his book *The Divine Conspiracy*, reminds us that Jesus is the smartest most capable person who has ever lived[17]. He could teach Einstein about physics and Silicon Valley about technology.

We are conditioned to see people from the ancient past as less evolved; not having the capabilities we have today. This type of thinking is deadly if we apply it to Jesus. He was transcendently brilliant. He knew how to regenerate the molecules in food. He could bring a leper's dead tissue back to life. He could manipulate the very atoms in water. It is not until we see Jesus as capable on this level that we will fully trust him with our lives.

Jesus' walking on water took place the very evening after his feeding the five thousand. The disciples would have been tapped out in their exhaustion and likely maxed out in their frustration at being caught in such a squall in the middle of the night. It is at this point that Jesus approached them, raising their terror level to new heights. He serenely appeared from out of the darkness, with the winds and waves thrashing all around him. What other than a ghost could do such a thing?

Only one of them kept his presence of mind enough to see the opportunity. Peter looked beyond the immediate conditions and realized that if Jesus could do it he could enable Peter to do it. It was only a matter of Jesus' willingness. Imagine how surreal that first step must have felt! It is easy to look down on Peter as he sank in the water, but no one else in that boat had the courage to step out and no one else had the joy of walking back to the boat with Jesus. One little noticed insight: when the disciples addressed Jesus as "the Son of God" it is the first time they did so in the book of Matthew. They realized that night, maybe for the first time, that Jesus was truly divine!

CORRELATION

Jesus knew in his spirit that this was what they were thinking in their hearts, and he said to them, "Why are you thinking these things?
  Mark 7:8

The disciples went and woke him, saying, "Lord, save us! We're going to drown!" He replied, "You of little faith, why are you so afraid?" Then he got up and rebuked the winds and the waves, and it was completely calm. The men were amazed and asked, "What kind of man is this? Even the winds and the waves obey him!"
  Matthew 8:25-27

RECITATION

Our Father in Heaven

Hallowed be Your Name

Your Kingdom come,

Your will be done,
 on earth as it is in Heaven.

Give us today our daily bread

Forgive us our debts,
 as we also have forgiven our debtors.

And lead us not into temptation,
 but deliver us from the evil one.

Matthew 6:9-13

APPLICATION

What has come to mind, either through the passage or in your reflection that you want to remember?

Healing A Blind Man

Passage: John 9:1-41

Meditation: John 9:18-38
Pause and Reflect Silently
Highlight Key Phrases
Look to and Lift up Christ

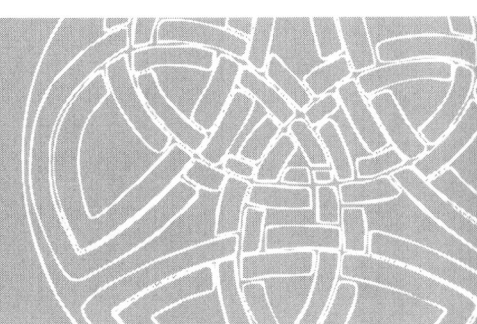

[18]They still did not believe that he had been blind and had received his sight until they sent for the man's parents. [19]"Is this your son?" they asked. "Is this the one you say was born blind? How is it that now he can see?"

[20]"We know he is our son," the parents answered, "and we know he was born blind. [21]But how he can see now, or who opened his eyes, we don't know. Ask him. He is of age; he will speak for himself."

[22]His parents said this because they were afraid of the Jewish leaders, who already had decided that anyone who acknowledged that Jesus was the Messiah would be put out of the synagogue. [23]That was why his parents said, "He is of age; ask him."

[24]A second time they summoned the man who had been blind. "Give glory to God by telling the truth," they said. "We know this man is a sinner." [25]He replied, "Whether he is a sinner or not, I

don't know. One thing I do know. I was blind but now I see!"

²⁶Then they asked him, "What did he do to you? How did he open your eyes?" ²⁷He answered, "I have told you already and you did not listen. Why do you want to hear it again? Do you want to become his disciples too?"

²⁸Then they hurled insults at him and said, "You are this fellow's disciple! We are disciples of Moses! ²⁹We know that God spoke to Moses, but as for this fellow, we don't even know where he comes from."

³⁰The man answered, "Now that is remarkable! You don't know where he comes from, yet he opened my eyes. ³¹We know that God does not listen to sinners. He listens to the godly person who does his will. ³²Nobody has ever heard of opening the eyes of a man born blind. ³³If this man were not from God, he could do nothing." ³⁴To this they replied, "You were steeped in sin at birth; how dare you lecture us!" And they threw him out.

³⁵Jesus heard that they had thrown him out, and when he found him, he said, "Do you believe in the Son of Man?" ³⁶"Who is he, sir?" the man asked. "Tell me so that I may believe in him." ³⁷Jesus said, "You have now seen him; in fact, he is the one speaking with you."

³⁸Then the man said, "Lord, I believe," and he worshiped him.

REFLECTION

"I once was blind but now I see." This line from the hymn *Amazing Grace*, was written by a former slave-trader who came to Christ in the 1700's. John Newton found his wording in this story of a blind man healed by Jesus, whose suffering was compounded by a lack of support from his family and mistreatment from the religious leaders of his time.

The common belief of the time was that disabilities like blindness came from a person's or family's sins. Such an idea is similar to the Hindu concept of Karma, which often leads people to leave others in misery because of the misguided belief that "they deserve what they are getting." Jesus rejects this idea. We live in a fallen world, but our individual disabilities and miseries cannot be fully explained by going back to our personal or family sin. There is something bigger going on: God has allowed suffering so that He can reveal the glory of his greater power and compassion.

The blind man is not just healed physically either; he is also restored inwardly through the difficult circumstances he faced *after* he was healed. Notice the courage he begins to show in rebuking the religious leaders for their willful blindness!

As the Light of the World, Jesus came to open the eyes of the blind about God and His purposes. The religious leaders should have been the first to see him for who he truly was, but they were upstaged by a man they could only sneer at.

We can find hope in knowing that God can meet people in their misery and heal them of not just their physical suffering but spiritual suffering as well. This world is filled with lies and superstitions that inflict pain. Those in power can compound the problem if they see in Jesus only a threat to their positions. They too can inflict suffering on those in their care. Yet as the blind man shows us, Jesus is able to use even these types of painful circumstances for our good.

CORRELATION

I, the Lord, have called you in righteousness; I will take hold of your hand. I will keep you and will make you to be a covenant for the people and a light for the Gentiles, to open eyes that are blind, to free captives from prison and to release from the dungeon those who sit in darkness.

Isaiah 42:6-7

RECITATION

Lord Jesus Christ, Son of God, have mercy on me, a sinner.

The Jesus Prayer

> Recite three times slowly.

APPLICATION

What has come to mind, either through the passage or in your reflection that you want to remember?

Healing A Possessed Man

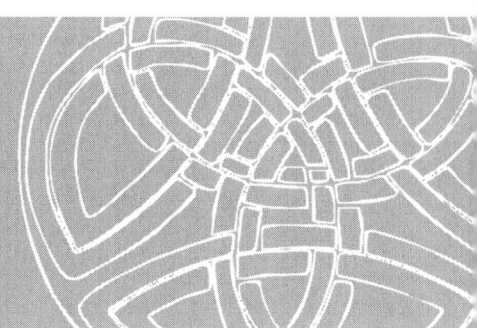

Passage: Mark 5:1-20

Meditation: Mark 5:1-20
Pause and Reflect Silently
Highlight Key Phrases
Look to and Lift up Christ

¹*They went across the lake to the region of the Gerasenes.' ²When Jesus got out of the boat, a man with an impure spirit came from the tombs to meet him.*

³*This man lived in the tombs, and no one could bind him anymore, not even with a chain. ⁴For he had often been chained hand and foot, but he tore the chains apart and broke the irons on his feet. No one was strong enough to subdue him. ⁵Night and day among the tombs and in the hills he would cry out and cut himself with stones.*

⁶*When he saw Jesus from a distance, he ran and fell on his knees in front of him. ⁷He shouted at the top of his voice, "What do you want with me, Jesus, Son of the Most High God? In God's name don't torture me!" ⁸For Jesus had said to him, "Come out of this man, you impure spirit!"*

⁹*Then Jesus asked him, "What is your name?" "My name is*

Legion," he replied, "for we are many." ¹⁰And he begged Jesus again and again not to send them out of the area.

¹¹A large herd of pigs was feeding on the nearby hillside. ¹²The demons begged Jesus, "Send us among the pigs; allow us to go into them." ¹³He gave them permission, and the impure spirits came out and went into the pigs. The herd, about two thousand in number, rushed down the steep bank into the lake and were drowned.

¹⁴Those tending the pigs ran off and reported this in the town and countryside, and the people went out to see what had happened. ¹⁵When they came to Jesus, they saw the man who had been possessed by the legion of demons, sitting there, dressed and in his right mind; and they were afraid.

¹⁶Those who had seen it told the people what had happened to the demon-possessed man—and told about the pigs as well. ¹⁷Then the people began to plead with Jesus to leave their region.

¹⁸As Jesus was getting into the boat, the man who had been demon-possessed begged to go with him. ¹⁹Jesus did not let him, but said, "Go home to your own people and tell them how much the Lord has done for you, and how he has had mercy on you." ²⁰So the man went away and began to tell in the Decapolis how much Jesus had done for him. And all the people were amazed.

REFLECTION

One day, Jesus and his disciples landed on a shore on the eastern side of the Galilee near a cemetery with surrounding caves. They were met by a man with superhuman strength who suffered horribly from demonic slavery and relational alienation. He had opened himself up to demonic influences and it had controlled his life for years. He had the scars to prove it.

This man had been so dehumanized and damaging to others that the cemetery was probably "the last place" he could stay. He was as alienated from God and others as you can get and still be officially alive. The good news is that the one person who had the ability and compassion this man needed came to his front door.

Jesus stood his ground as that demon-possessed man ran full throttle at him screaming, "What do you have to do with me?" The demons tried to gain authority over Jesus by speaking his name but Jesus easily rebuked them and gained their name: Legion. He then cast the demons into a herd of pigs which immediately ran full throttle into the sea.

When we think of sin we usually think of it as a choice. We should also think of it as a corrosive: it eats away at our humanity and opens us up to demonic oppression. This corrosion damages and distances us from God and others, and makes us truly "unclean" before God. Yet it does not necessarily make us *unlovable* to God!

When we think of authority we need to remind ourselves that Jesus has authoritative power over every area of life (Matt 28:18). He could calm the sea (Mark 4:35-41) and cast out a demon with just a word. He uses that authority to liberate and restore people into their "right minds,"--even those who are suffering from their own sinful choices.

And it is not just spiritual restoration that Jesus brings. He also brought relational restoration into that man's life by sending him back to his hometown to reconnect with those who knew him before his encounter with Jesus. Imagine what God's serene peace and restored relationships would have felt like to that former demoniac.

CORRELATION

But if it is by the Spirit of God that I drive out demons, then the kingdom of God has come upon you. Or again, how can anyone enter a strong man's house and carry off his possessions unless he first ties up the strong man? Then he can plunder his house.

Matthew 12:28-29

[Jesus is] far above all rule and authority, power and dominion, and every name that is invoked, not only in the present age but also in the one to come. And God placed all things under his feet and appointed him to be head over everything for the church...

Ephesians 1:21-22

RECITATION

I believe in God the Father, Almighty Maker of heaven and earth.

And in Jesus Christ his only Son our Lord; who was conceived by the Holy Spirit,

born of the Virgin Mary, suffered under Pontius Pilate, was crucified, dead, and buried; he descended into hell; the third day he rose again from the dead;

He ascended into heaven, and sits on the right hand of God the Father Almighty; from there he shall come to judge the living and the dead.

I believe in the Holy Spirit; the holy Christian Church; the communion of saints; the forgiveness of sins; the resurrection of the body; and the life everlasting. AMEN.

The Apostle's Creed

APPLICATION

What has come to mind, either through the passage or in your reflection that you want to remember?

Raising Lazarus

Passage: John 11:1-57

Meditation: John 11:17-37
Pause and Reflect Silently
Highlight Key Phrases
Look to and Lift up Christ

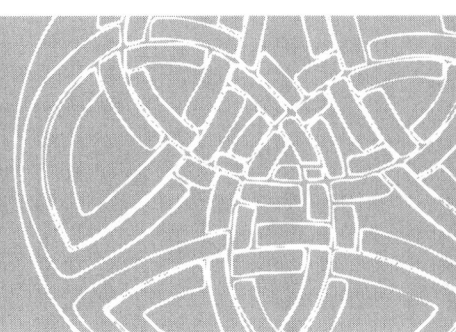

¹⁷*On his arrival, Jesus found that Lazarus had already been in the tomb for four days. ¹⁸Now Bethany was less than two miles from Jerusalem, ¹⁹and many Jews had come to Martha and Mary to comfort them in the loss of their brother. ²⁰When Martha heard that Jesus was coming, she went out to meet him, but Mary stayed at home.*

²¹*"Lord," Martha said to Jesus, "if you had been here, my brother would not have died. ²²But I know that even now God will give you whatever you ask." ²³Jesus said to her, "Your brother will rise again."*

²⁴*Martha answered, "I know he will rise again in the resurrection at the last day." ²⁵Jesus said to her, "I am the resurrection and the life. The one who believes in me will live, even though they die; ²⁶and whoever lives by believing in me will never die. Do you believe this?"*

²⁷"Yes, Lord," she replied, "I believe that you are the Messiah, the Son of God, who is to come into the world."

²⁸After she had said this, she went back and called her sister Mary aside. "The Teacher is here," she said, "and is asking for you." ²⁹When Mary heard this, she got up quickly and went to him. ³⁰Now Jesus had not yet entered the village, but was still at the place where Martha had met him. ³¹When the Jews who had been with Mary in the house, comforting her, noticed how quickly she got up and went out, they followed her, supposing she was going to the tomb to mourn there.

³²When Mary reached the place where Jesus was and saw him, she fell at his feet and said, "Lord, if you had been here, my brother would not have died." ³³When Jesus saw her weeping, and the Jews who had come along with her also weeping, he was deeply moved in spirit and troubled. ³⁴"Where have you laid him?" he asked. "Come and see, Lord," they replied.

³⁵Jesus wept.

³⁶Then the Jews said, "See how he loved him!"

³⁷But some of them said, "Could not he who opened the eyes of the blind man have kept this man from dying?"

REFLECTION

Earlier in his ministry, Jesus had raised Jairus' daughter (Luke 8:41ff) and a widow's son (Luke 7:11-17) from the dead. He had responded immediately in both cases. Here he purposely waits, and his waiting leads us into a deeper understanding of both him and his power over life and death.

Jesus first reassures his disciples that this episode in Lazarus' life will not *end* in death, but we see that it still goes *through* death. Because of his comments, Christians can now view death as a "sleep" in which we rest from our earthly toil and not as a "sentence" in which we enter into sin's punishment.

Jesus next strengthens Martha and Mary when he arrives in Bethany. He does so by reasoning with Martha and empathizing with Mary. Martha's confidence in the future resurrection was a sign of her faith in Jesus' teaching. Mary's confidence that Jesus would share in her grief was a sign of her faith in Jesus' heart. Both needed Jesus' ministry to grow through the grief of losing their brother.

Notice that Martha draws out some of Jesus' clearest insights on the resurrection, while Mary draws out his deepest expression of compassion that we have in the Gospels. They *together* reveal how Jesus helps us through the painful traumas of life. In our pain, we need to reason with him through his truth *and* we need to grieve with him through his empathy.

Jesus lastly demonstrates that his authority extends even into the realm of the dead by calling Lazarus back from the grave. Lazarus had been dead four days: his brain had lost its functioning and his body had begun decomposing. Yet with a word, Jesus called him back in his fully restored mind and body. Jesus is the source and channel of God's life, in all its power. When we are united with him by faith we enter into the "stream" of his life which will one day open up into the ocean of eternity at the future resurrection. We can know today that we will truly never die!

CORRELATION

I know that my redeemer lives, and that in the end he will stand on the earth. And after my skin has been destroyed, yet in my flesh I will see God... Job 19:25-26

Jesus said to her, "I am the resurrection and the life. The one who believes in me will live, even though they die; and whoever lives by believing in me will never die. Do you believe this?" John 11:25-26

RECITATION

O Father, light up
 the small duties of this day's life;

May they shine
 with the beauty of Your countenance.

May we believe that glory can dwell
 in the commonest task of every day.

Augustine of Hippo

APPLICATION

What has come to mind, either through the passage or in your reflection that you want to remember?

The Last Supper

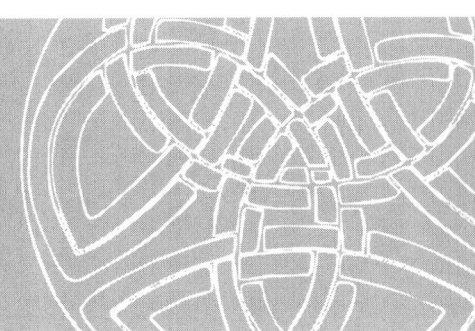

Passage: Luke 22:1-46

Meditation: Luke 22:1-23
Pause and Reflect Silently
Highlight Key Phrases
Look to and Lift up Christ

¹*Now the Festival of Unleavened Bread, called the Passover, was approaching,* ²*and the chief priests and the teachers of the law were looking for some way to get rid of Jesus, for they were afraid of the people.*

³*Then Satan entered Judas, called Iscariot, one of the Twelve.* ⁴*And Judas went to the chief priests and the officers of the temple guard and discussed with them how he might betray Jesus.* ⁵*They were delighted and agreed to give him money.* ⁶*He consented, and watched for an opportunity to hand Jesus over to them when no crowd was present.*

⁷*Then came the day of Unleavened Bread on which the Passover lamb had to be sacrificed.* ⁸*Jesus sent Peter and John, saying, "Go and make preparations for us to eat the Passover."* ⁹*"Where do you want us to prepare for it?" they asked.*

¹⁰*He replied, "As you enter the city, a man carrying a jar of water will meet you. Follow him to the house that he enters,*

¹¹*and say to the owner of the house, 'The Teacher asks: Where is the guest room, where I may eat the Passover with my disciples?'* ¹²*He will show you a large room upstairs, all furnished. Make preparations there."* ¹³*They left and found things just as Jesus had told them. So they prepared the Passover.*

¹⁴*When the hour came, Jesus and his apostles reclined at the table.* ¹⁵*And he said to them, "I have eagerly desired to eat this Passover with you before I suffer.* ¹⁶*For I tell you, I will not eat it again until it finds fulfillment in the kingdom of God."*

¹⁷*After taking the cup, he gave thanks and said, "Take this and divide it among you.* ¹⁸*For I tell you I will not drink again from the fruit of the vine until the kingdom of God comes."*

¹⁹*And he took bread, gave thanks and broke it, and gave it to them, saying, "This is my body given for you; do this in remembrance of me."*

²⁰*In the same way, after the supper he took the cup, saying, "This cup is the new covenant in my blood, which is poured out for you.* ²¹*But the hand of him who is going to betray me is with mine on the table.* ²²*The Son of Man will go as it has been decreed. But woe to that man who betrays him!"* ²³*They began to question among themselves which of them it might be who would do this.*

REFLECTION

By Jesus' time, the Jewish people had been celebrating the Passover Meal for *fourteen centuries*. It had always been followed by the seven-day Feast of Unleavened Bread. Through all of Israel's victories and defeats, from the early days under Joshua, through the glory days of David and Solomon, to the exile into Babylon and return; through the years of domination under the Assyrians, Babylonians, Persians, Greeks and Romans, one of the only constants in their national life was the celebration of Passover.

Its origin went back to the night the Jewish people shared in the meal of a lamb, while they waited for God to deliver them from their slavery under the Egyptians. They could do nothing to save themselves but they were called to obey God by placing the blood of the Lamb on their door-frames and then partaking of the Lamb together. They had been given a number of instructions, one of which was to take all of the leaven, or yeast, out of their homes as preparation. They were to do this with deathly seriousness and a sense of urgency. It was the way the people personally purified themselves from the influences of the culture around them so they could dedicate themselves in a fresh way to God.

The Passover may have been the most important tradition in forming the identity of the Jewish people. Yet Jesus redefined its meaning that last night. The Jewish people had always looked back to the Exodus from Egypt when they celebrated the Meal. Jesus revealed that it had an even greater significance: it looked forward to his own death on the cross. It was a foreshadowing of His work of salvation, which would be founded on the sacrifice of his body and blood.

Further, the Exodus informs our understanding of our salvation today. We have been delivered from the oppression and slavery of sin, not by anything we have done for ourselves, but by the powerful hand of God and the covering sacrifice of His perfect Lamb: Jesus.

CORRELATION

Your boasting is not good. Don't you know that a little yeast leavens the whole batch of dough? Get rid of the old yeast, so that you may be a new unleavened batch—as you really are. For Christ, our Passover lamb, has been sacrificed. Therefore let us keep the Festival, not with the old bread leavened with malice and wickedness, but with the unleavened bread of sincerity and truth.

1 Corinthians 5:6-8

RECITATION

LORD, MAKE ME AN INSTRUMENT OF YOUR PEACE,

where there is hatred, let me sow love,

where there is injury, pardon,

where there is discord, may I bring harmony,

where there is error, may I bring truth,

where there is doubt, may I bring faith,

where there is despair, may I bring hope,

where there is darkness, may I bring light,

and where there is sadness, may I bring joy.

O Divine Master,

grant that I may not so much seek

to be consoled, as to console,

to be understood, as to understand,

to be loved, as to love.

for it is in giving that we receive;

it is in pardoning that we are pardoned;

and it is in dying that we are born into eternal life.

Francis of Assisi

APPLICATION

What has come to mind, either through the passage or in your reflection that you want to remember?

Arrest and Trial

Passage: John 18:1-40

Meditation: John 18:29-40
Pause and Reflect Silently
Highlight Key Phrases
Look to and Lift up Christ

²⁹*So Pilate came out to them and asked, "What charges are you bringing against this man?"*

³⁰*"If he were not a criminal," they replied, "we would not have handed him over to you." ³¹Pilate said, "Take him yourselves and judge him by your own law."*

"But we have no right to execute anyone," they objected. ³²This took place to fulfill what Jesus had said about the kind of death he was going to die. ³³Pilate then went back inside the palace, summoned Jesus and asked him, "Are you the king of the Jews?" ³⁴"Is that your own idea," Jesus asked, "or did others talk to you about me?"

³⁵*"Am I a Jew?" Pilate replied. "Your own people and chief priests handed you over to me. What is it you have done?"*

³⁶*Jesus said, "My kingdom is not of this world. If it were, my servants would fight to prevent my arrest by the Jewish leaders. But now my kingdom is from another place." ³⁷"You are a king, then!" said Pilate.*

Jesus answered, "You say that I am a king. In fact, the reason I was born and came into the world is to testify to the truth. Everyone on the side of truth listens to me."

³⁸"What is truth?" retorted Pilate. With this he went out again to the Jews gathered there and said, "I find no basis for a charge against him. ³⁹But it is your custom for me to release to you one prisoner at the time of the Passover. Do you want me to release 'the king of the Jews'?"

⁴⁰They shouted back, "No, not him! Give us Barabbas!" Now Barabbas had taken part in an uprising.

REFLECTION

Some want to see Jesus as an idealistic reformer overwhelmed by circumstances, yet nothing in our record supports this idea. Jesus was not a victim of circumstances but a masterful shaper of events.

We see this clearly in the events of Jesus' last week. Every moment was significant. Old Testament prophecies were being fulfilled. Jesus was displaying a command of himself and every situation that inspired people's awe, even as events seemed to increasingly spiral out of control.

The Jewish political parties were working behind the scenes to find some way to discredit and kill him. Always at odds with each other, they had *finally* found unity in their hostility towards Jesus. And his closest followers were too fearful, immature and impulsive to be of any help to him. Yet through it all, Jesus kept his composure. His discussion with Pilate on the nature of his kingdom and of truth displays a calm and wisdom that still resonate two thousand years later.

We shouldn't miss the irony either: Jesus, in all of his perfections and nobility, brought out the imperfections and savagery fallen human beings are capable of. From the traitor Judas to the calloused High Priest, on through prideful Peter to the calculating Pilate, humankind's sin is on full display.

As we read and re-read this story, we need to identify with and own up to their sin because their sin is our sin. We are prone to the same reactions and we would not have been any less selfish or fearful. The more deeply we accept these truths the more wonderful and beautiful Jesus will become! He didn't come to save a bunch of misguided do-gooders: he came to save selfish, short-sighted, calloused, and cruel sinners. He knew how deep and dark our sin really is and yet he came to save us in his tender mercy and amazing grace!

CORRELATION

The heart is deceitful above all things and beyond cure. Who can understand it?
   Jeremiah 17:9

Jesus would not entrust himself to them, for he knew all people. He did not need any testimony about mankind, for he knew what was in each person.
   John 2:24-25

RECITATION

Thanks be to you, our Lord Jesus Christ,

For all the benefits you have given us,

For all the pains and insults you have borne for us.

Most merciful Redeemer, Friend, and Brother,

May we know you more clearly,

Love you more dearly,

And follow you more nearly:

Forever and ever. AMEN

Richard Chichester

APPLICATION

What has come to mind, either through the passage or in your reflection that you want to remember?

The Crucifixion

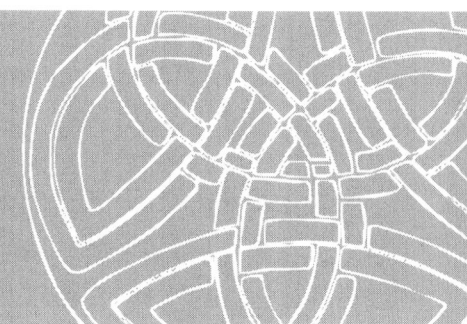

Passage: John 19:1-42

Meditation: John 19: 1-18
Pause and Reflect Silently
Highlight Key Phrases
Look to and Lift up Christ

¹*Then Pilate took Jesus and had him flogged. ²The soldiers twisted together a crown of thorns and put it on his head. They clothed him in a purple robe ³and went up to him again and again, saying, "Hail, king of the Jews!" And they slapped him in the face.*

⁴*Once more Pilate came out and said to the Jews gathered there, "Look, I am bringing him out to you to let you know that I find no basis for a charge against him." ⁵When Jesus came out wearing the crown of thorns and the purple robe, Pilate said to them, "Here is the man!"*

⁶*As soon as the chief priests and their officials saw him, they shouted, "Crucify! Crucify!" But Pilate answered, "You take him and crucify him. As for me, I find no basis for a charge against him."*

⁷*The Jewish leaders insisted, "We have a law, and according to that law he must die, because he claimed to be the Son of God."*

⁸When Pilate heard this, he was even more afraid, ⁹and he went back inside the palace. "Where do you come from?" he asked Jesus, but Jesus gave him no answer. ¹⁰"Do you refuse to speak to me?" Pilate said. "Don't you realize I have power either to free you or to crucify you?"

¹¹Jesus answered, "You would have no power over me if it were not given to you from above. Therefore the one who handed me over to you is guilty of a greater sin."

¹²From then on, Pilate tried to set Jesus free, but the Jewish leaders kept shouting, "If you let this man go, you are no friend of Caesar. Anyone who claims to be a king opposes Caesar."

¹³When Pilate heard this, he brought Jesus out and sat down on the judge's seat at a place known as the Stone Pavement (which in Aramaic is Gabbatha). ¹⁴It was the day of Preparation of the Passover; it was about noon.

"Here is your king," Pilate said to the Jews. ¹⁵But they shouted, "Take him away! Take him away! Crucify him!" "Shall I crucify your king?" Pilate asked. "We have no king but Caesar," the chief priests answered. ¹⁶Finally Pilate handed him over to them to be crucified.

So the soldiers took charge of Jesus. ¹⁷Carrying his own cross, he went out to the place of the Skull (which in Aramaic is called Golgotha). ¹⁸There they crucified him, and with him two others—one on each side and Jesus in the middle.

REFLECTION

The Jewish people were the most educated and moral people in the ancient world. Having been given the gifts of the Torah (The Pentateuch, or Five Books of Moses), the prophets and the godly leaders of their past, it seems unbelievable that they could look right at Jesus and not see their Messiah. Yet, framed in our terms today, they unjustly and cruelly lynched the wisest, most caring, person who has ever lived.

As the Jewish leaders conspired with the Roman leaders to crucify Jesus their envy and selfishness spiraled down into human cruelty and depravity. John makes the point that the Gentile Pontius Pilate did more to try to save Jesus than the Jewish leaders of his time. He didn't do so out of compassion though. Once he realized he couldn't sway the crowd to free Jesus, he abandoned an innocent man to the tortures and humiliations of the cross. And he rubbed it in the Jewish leaders' faces by having "King of the Jews" written on a sign over his cross. As cynical as it was, Pilate displayed the truth of Jesus' true identity.

The Gospel writers do not describe the crucifixion in detail: they all knew what happened. Movies like the *Passion of the Christ* help us better grasp how terrible it was. Yet Jesus endured it all and when he uttered "It is finished," it was not just his life and physical suffering that came to an end: the Old Testament era of animal sacrifice "officially" ended as well. Jesus, the perfect, innocent Lamb, had been slain. There was no longer any need for continued sacrifices.

One glimmer of hope on that day was the courage a few disciples showed in taking care of the dead body of Jesus. Both Joseph and Nicodemus had much to lose in identifying with Jesus after his death, but they both stepped out and treated his dead body with the dignity it deserved.

CORRELATION

My God, my God, why have you forsaken me? Why are you so far from saving me, so far from my cries of anguish? My God, I cry out by day, but you do not answer, by night, but I find no rest.
Psalm 22:1-2

For by one sacrifice he has made perfect forever those who are being made holy.
Hebrews 10:14

RECITATION

Lord, whatever this day may bring

Your name be praised.

Be gracious to me and help me.

Grant me strength to bear whatever you may send,
   and let not fear overrule me.

I trust your grace and commit my life wholly into your
   hands.

Whether I live or whether I die, I am with you.

And you are with me,

O my Lord and my God.

Lord, I wait for your salvation,
   and for the coming of your kingdom. AMEN.

Dietrich Bonhoeffer

APPLICATION

What has come to mind, either through the passage or in your reflection that you want to remember?

The Resurrection

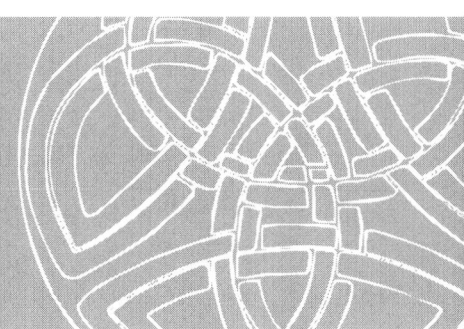

Passage: John 20:1 – 21:25

Meditation: John 20:19-31
Pause and Reflect Silently
Highlight Key Phrases
Look to and Lift up Christ

[19]On the evening of that first day of the week, when the disciples were together, with the doors locked for fear of the Jewish leaders, Jesus came and stood among them and said, "Peace be with you!"

[20]After he said this, he showed them his hands and side. The disciples were overjoyed when they saw the Lord.

[21]Again Jesus said, "Peace be with you! As the Father has sent me, I am sending you." [22]And with that he breathed on them and said, "Receive the Holy Spirit.

[23]If you forgive anyone's sins, their sins are forgiven; if you do not forgive them, they are not forgiven."

[24]Now Thomas (also known as Didymus), one of the Twelve, was not with the disciples when Jesus came. [25]So the other disciples told him, "We have seen the Lord!"

But he said to them, "Unless I see the nail marks in his hands and put my finger where the nails were, and put my hand into his side, I will not believe."

²⁶A week later his disciples were in the house again, and Thomas was with them. Though the doors were locked, Jesus came and stood among them and said, "Peace be with you!" ²⁷Then he said to Thomas, "Put your finger here; see my hands. Reach out your hand and put it into my side. Stop doubting and believe."

²⁸Thomas said to him, "My Lord and my God!"

²⁹Then Jesus told him, "Because you have seen me, you have believed; blessed are those who have not seen and yet have believed."

³⁰Jesus performed many other signs in the presence of his disciples, which are not recorded in this book. ³¹But these are written that you may believe that Jesus is the Messiah, the Son of God, and that by believing you may have life in his name.

REFLECTION

Christianity began where religious obligation ended: in the resurrection of Jesus Christ! The resurrection of Jesus Christ is one of the most well documented events of the ancient world. It changes everything about the way we look at life as well as the afterlife. C.S. Lewis said "Christianity is a statement which, if false, is of *no* importance, and if true, of infinite importance. The one thing it cannot be is moderately important."[18]

The stories of the resurrection paint a picture of Jesus' followers as devastated, in shock and completely unprepared for what they experienced. Jesus reveals himself privately to some of them, to groups at other times, often asking for something simple like a piece of broiled fish. In every instance you sense him reassuring and slowly restoring his followers.

He is not recorded to have revealed himself to any of the religious or political authorities who had crucified him. The privilege of seeing him on this side of the grave was a personal gift he gave to his followers, many of whom would lose their lives for their faithfulness to him.

As Christians we stake our entire lives on the honesty of those original followers. There is ample evidence to support their witness and no compelling evidence to deny them. Why would a group of peasants and fishermen proclaim a message they knew would only get them in trouble and most likely lead to their deaths, if they knew it to be a lie or just wish-fulfillment?

For those of us who will not see Jesus before we stand before him in heaven, he gives a promise: "Blessed are those who have not seen and yet have believed." Let us remember that we are Easter people and that the final word on life will be a thunderous Hallelujah to the Lord Jesus Christ, resurrected from the dead and reigning in glory from heaven!

CORRELATION

But Christ has indeed been raised from the dead, the firstfruits of those who have fallen asleep. For since death came through a man, the resurrection of the dead comes also through a man. For as in Adam all die, so in Christ all will be made alive.
   1 Corinthians 15:20-22

RECITATION

GOD, GRANT ME THE SERENITY
  to accept the things I cannot change;

Courage to change the things I can and
  the wisdom to know the difference.

To live one day at a time;
  enjoying one moment at a time;

Accepting hardship as the pathway to peace.

To take, as He did, this sinful world as it is, not as I would have it.

Trusting that He will make all things right if I surrender to His Will.

That I may be reasonably happy in this life and supremely happy with You forever in the next. AMEN

Reinhold Neibuhr

APPLICATION

What has come to mind, either through the passage or in your reflection that you want to remember?

The Ascension

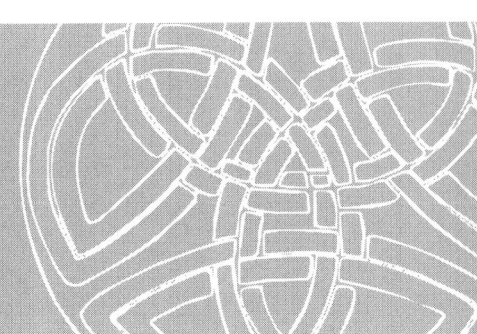

Passage: Acts 1:1-11

Meditation: Acts 1:1-11
Pause and Reflect Silently
Highlight Key Phrases
Look to and Lift up Christ

¹In my former book, Theophilus, I wrote about all that Jesus began to do and to teach ²until the day he was taken up to heaven, after giving instructions through the Holy Spirit to the apostles he had chosen.

³After his suffering, he presented himself to them and gave many convincing proofs that he was alive. He appeared to them over a period of forty days and spoke about the kingdom of God.

⁴On one occasion, while he was eating with them, he gave them this command: "Do not leave Jerusalem, but wait for the gift my Father promised, which you have heard me speak about. ⁵For John baptized with water, but in a few days you will be baptized with the Holy Spirit."

⁶Then they gathered around him and asked him, "Lord, are you at this time going to restore the kingdom to Israel?"

⁷He said to them: *"It is not for you to know the times or dates the Father has set by his own authority.*

⁸*But you will receive power when the Holy Spirit comes on you; and you will be my witnesses in Jerusalem, and in all Judea and Samaria, and to the ends of the earth."*

⁹*After he said this, he was taken up before their very eyes, and a cloud hid him from their sight.*

¹⁰*They were looking intently up into the sky as he was going, when suddenly two men dressed in white stood beside them.* ¹¹*"Men of Galilee," they said, "why do you stand here looking into the sky? This same Jesus, who has been taken from you into heaven, will come back in the same way you have seen him go into heaven."*

REFLECTION

The Book of Acts was written by Luke and again addressed to Theophilus. He mentions that Jesus revealed himself to his followers on many different occasions over a forty day period of time. Jesus had begun his ministry with a forty day period of preparation in the desert *after* being baptized by the Spirit. Jesus continued his ministry through his disciples by preparing them over a forty day period *before* their baptism in the Spirit.

Jesus focused on the Kingdom of God and the gift of the Holy Spirit during that period. There is disagreement among scholars about the meaning of Jesus' comments about Israel and the Kingdom. Is he saying there will be or will not be an earthly Kingdom established for the Jewish people?

Jesus leaves the question unanswered. He redirects his followers' attention to the work at hand: they are going to become his authoritative witnesses to the world. Their focus should not be on Jewish Israel but on the entire world.

His followers are given three lasting gifts: 1) God's promises in Jesus Christ. 2) God's power in the Holy Spirit. 3) God's purpose in reaching the entire world. All three will continue in force until the time Jesus returns in glory. His message will go out and His Spirit will ensure its ultimate victory and effectiveness through his followers' trust and obedience.

The passage ends with Jesus' ascension into heaven. The cloud that hid Jesus was most likely the Shekinah, which was the visible manifestation of God's presence, glory and blessing. It led Israel through the desert and hovered over the tabernacle. Later it fell powerfully upon the Temple built by Solomon (1 Kings 8) only to leave the Temple for good in the time of Ezekiel (Ez. 10). It had not been seen for hundreds of years until the moment when Jesus was baptized by John. From that time on, the Shekinah glory cloud of God would always be found with Jesus.

CORRELATION

While Aaron was speaking to the whole Israelite community, they looked toward the desert, and there was the glory of the Lord appearing in the cloud.

Exodus 16:10

...the priests could not perform their service because of the cloud, for the glory of the Lord filled his temple.

1 Kings 8:11

RECITATION

Father, we give you thanks for all the gifts you freely bestow on us. For the beauty and wonder of your creation, in earth and sky and sea, Lord, we thank you.

For our daily food and drink, our homes and families, and our friends, Lord, we thank you.

For minds to think, and hearts to love, and hands to serve, Lord, we thank you. For health and strength to work, and leisure to rest and play, Lord, we thank you.

For the brave and courageous, who are patient in suffering and faithful in adversity, Lord, we thank you.

For the communion of saints, in all times and places, Lord, we thank you.

Above all, we give you thanks for the great mercies and promises given to us in Christ Jesus our Lord; to him be praise and glory, with you, O Father, and the Holy Spirit, now and forever. AMEN.

APPLICATION

What has come to mind, either through the passage or in your reflection that you want to remember?

The Day of Pentecost

Passage: Acts 2:1-47

Meditation: Acts 2:22-41
Pause and Reflect Silently
Highlight Key Phrases
Look to and Lift up Christ

²²"*Fellow Israelites, listen to this: Jesus of Nazareth was a man accredited by God to you by miracles, wonders and signs, which God did among you through him, as you yourselves know.* ²³*This man was handed over to you by God's deliberate plan and foreknowledge; and you, with the help of wicked men, put him to death by nailing him to the cross.*

²⁴*But God raised him from the dead, freeing him from the agony of death, because it was impossible for death to keep its hold on him.* ²⁵*David said about him:*

"'I saw the Lord always before me. Because he is at my right hand, I will not be shaken. ²⁶*Therefore my heart is glad and my tongue rejoices; my body also will rest in hope,* ²⁷*because you will not abandon me to the realm of the dead, you will not let your holy one see decay.* ²⁸*You have made known to me the paths of life; you will fill me with joy in your presence.'*

²⁹"Fellow Israelites, I can tell you confidently that the patriarch David died and was buried, and his tomb is here to this day. ³⁰But he was a prophet and knew that God had promised him on oath that he would place one of his descendants on his throne. ³¹Seeing what was to come, he spoke of the resurrection of the Messiah, that he was not abandoned to the realm of the dead, nor did his body see decay.

³²God has raised this Jesus to life, and we are all witnesses of it. ³³Exalted to the right hand of God, he has received from the Father the promised Holy Spirit and has poured out what you now see and hear. ³⁴For David did not ascend to heaven, and yet he said,

"'The Lord said to my Lord: "Sit at my right hand ³⁵until I make your enemies a footstool for your feet."' ³⁶"Therefore let all Israel be assured of this: God has made this Jesus, whom you crucified, both Lord and Messiah."

³⁷When the people heard this, they were cut to the heart and said to Peter and the other apostles, "Brothers, what shall we do?"

³⁸Peter replied, "Repent and be baptized, every one of you, in the name of Jesus Christ for the forgiveness of your sins. And you will receive the gift of the Holy Spirit. ³⁹The promise is for you and your children and for all who are far off—for all whom the Lord our God will call."

⁴⁰With many other words he warned them; and he pleaded with them, "Save yourselves from this corrupt generation."

⁴¹Those who accepted his message were baptized, and about three thousand were added to their number that day.

REFLECTION

The word Pentecost comes from the Greek word "fiftieth." It referred to the Jewish Festival of First Fruits which was later called the Feast of Weeks; it was to take place seven weeks after the Day of Passover (1 +(7x7)= 50 days).

By Jesus' time, Pentecost had become the anniversary of the giving of the Law to Moses on Mt Sinai. Thus, on the first anniversary of the "Old" Covenant after Jesus' resurrection, God poured out His Spirit to begin the era of the New Covenant. When God gave His Law the moment was filled with the sounds of thunder and trumpets and the Lord descended on the mountain as a fire (Ex 19). When God gave His Spirit on Pentecost the moment was filled with the sound of a violent wind and He descended on the disciples in tongues of fire.

Thousands of Jewish people and converts from all over the Roman Empire came to celebrate Passover and stay for Pentecost. As the people mixed and mingled with one another that Pentecost morning they became conscious of an unexplainably loud sound of wind; as they approached its source they saw people with undulating flames above their heads. As they drew nearer they heard their own, as well as others', languages being spoken in praises to God. Everyone present heard their own native tongues spoken by this small group of Galileans. Imagine the sense of astonishment and spine-tingling shock they must have felt!

The beginning of the New Covenant included the first sermon given by Peter. In it he explains how this moment fulfilled God's promise to pour out His Spirit on all His people, not just His leaders. For them to get the full message though, they needed to be convicted about "Jesus of Nazareth... whom you crucified." It is essential to see that God's Spirit is only given to those who are willing to humble themselves enough to take responsibility for their part in Christ's death.

CORRELATION

...there was thunder and lightning, with a thick cloud over the mountain and a very loud trumpet blast. Everyone in the camp trembled. Then Moses led the people out of the camp to meet with God and they stood at the foot of the mountain. Mt Sinai was covered with smoke, because the Lord descended on it in fire. The smoke billowed up from it like smoke from a furnace and the whole mountain trembled violently. As the sound of the trumpet grew louder and louder, Moses spoke and the voice of God answered him.

Exodus 19:16-19

RECITATION

Lord, you have been our dwelling place throughout all generations.

Before the mountains were born or you brought forth the universe, from everlasting to everlasting, you are God.

Forgive us our sins that we might not be consumed by your anger.

Teach us to number our days that we may gain a heart of wisdom.

Satisfy us in the morning with your unfailing love, that we may sing for joy and be glad in all our days.

Heal us and restore us from our afflictions, Lord, for this world is filled with many troubles.

May your favor rest upon us, and may the work of our hands be established by You, Father.

A prayer based on Psalm 90

APPLICATION

What has come to mind, either through the passage or in your reflection that you want to remember?

Growth and Persecution

Passage: Acts 3:1-4:37

Meditation: Acts 4:23-37
Pause and Reflect Silently
Highlight Key Phrases
Look to and Lift up Christ

²³*On their release, Peter and John went back to their own people and reported all that the chief priests and the elders had said to them.*

²⁴*When they heard this, they raised their voices together in prayer to God. "Sovereign Lord," they said, "you made the heavens and the earth and the sea, and everything in them.* ²⁵*You spoke by the Holy Spirit through the mouth of your servant, our father David:*

"'Why do the nations rage and the peoples plot in vain?

²⁶*The kings of the earth rise up and the rulers band together against the Lord and against his anointed one.'*

²⁷*Indeed Herod and Pontius Pilate met together with the Gentiles and the people of Israel in this city to conspire against your holy servant Jesus, whom you anointed.* ²⁸*They did what your power and will had decided beforehand*

*should happen. *²⁹*Now, Lord, consider their threats and enable your servants to speak your word with great boldness. *³⁰*Stretch out your hand to heal and perform signs and wonders through the name of your holy servant Jesus."*

³¹*After they prayed, the place where they were meeting was shaken. And they were all filled with the Holy Spirit and spoke the word of God boldly.*

³²*All the believers were one in heart and mind. No one claimed that any of their possessions was their own, but they shared everything they had. *³³*With great power the apostles continued to testify to the resurrection of the Lord Jesus. And God's grace was so powerfully at work in them all *³⁴*that there were no needy persons among them. For from time to time those who owned land or houses sold them, brought the money from the sales *³⁵*and put it at the apostles' feet, and it was distributed to anyone who had need.*

³⁶*Joseph, a Levite from Cyprus, whom the apostles called Barnabas (which means "son of encouragement"), *³⁷*sold a field he owned and brought the money and put it at the apostles' feet.*

REFLECTION

There are three seasons of miracles recorded in the Bible. The first took place under the leadership of Moses and Joshua (The books of Exodus through Joshua). The second took place through the ministries of Elijah and Elisha (1 Kings 17 to 2 Kings 13). The third took place through the ministries of Jesus and His Apostles.

The Apostles are clearly transformed men. Having spent time with the resurrected Christ and been filled with the Holy Spirit they had both the Scriptural understanding and spiritual boldness that they needed to witness to the Jewish people in the very same city where Jesus was crucified.

The opportunity to witness came about when Peter and John healed the beggar "in the name of Jesus." One's name referred to one's reputation and/or authority. As we have seen, authority is a form of power that is activated with a word, or command. Peter made it clear that they had no human power to heal but it was Jesus' power that was being manifested through them before the eyes of others. The healing was a manifestation of the presence and power of Christ. Jesus was truly continuing his ministry through the Apostles.

Peter's sermon is founded in Old Testament truths and speaks directly to those responsible for Jesus' crucifixion. He promises refreshment to those who return to God through Christ but judgment for those who do not.

One of the lessons of Christian history is that there is a backlash to every genuine spiritual advance. The Jewish authorities began to realize that they had not silenced the Jesus movement by crucifying its founder. They had hoped that they could intimidate the Apostles and make them go away. But those original followers responded to the threats with praise and prayer and set the example for all the Christians who would face similar challenges after them.

CORRELATION

The apostles performed many signs and wonders among the people. And all the believers used to meet together in Solomon's Colonnade. No one else dared join them, even though they were highly regarded by the people.

Acts 5:12-13

Blessed is the one who trusts in the Lord, who does not look to the proud, to those who turn aside to false gods. Many, Lord my God, are the wonders you have done, the things you planned for us. None can compare with you; were I to speak and tell of your deeds, they would be too many to declare.

Psalm 40:4-5

RECITATION

Our Father in Heaven

Hallowed be Your Name

Your Kingdom come,

Your will be done,
  on earth as it is in Heaven.

Give us today our daily bread

Forgive us our debts,
  as we also have forgiven our debtors.

And lead us not into temptation,
  but deliver us from the evil one.

Matthew 6:9-13

APPLICATION

What has come to mind, either through the passage or in your reflection that you want to remember?

The First Martyr

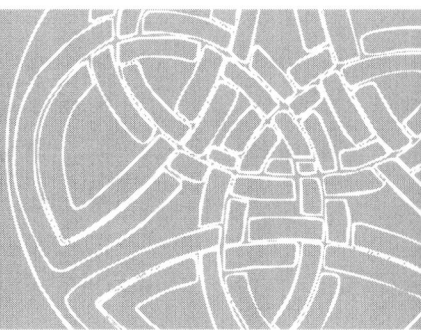

Passage: Acts 6:8-8:8

Meditation: Acts 7:39-42, 44-60
Pause and Reflect Silently
Highlight Key Phrases
Look to and Lift up Christ

³⁹*"But our ancestors refused to obey [Moses]. Instead, they rejected him and in their hearts turned back to Egypt. ⁴⁰They told Aaron, 'Make us gods who will go before us. As for this fellow Moses who led us out of Egypt—we don't know what has happened to him!' ⁴¹That was the time they made an idol in the form of a calf. They brought sacrifices to it and reveled in what their own hands had made. ⁴²But God turned away from them and gave them over to the worship of the sun, moon and stars...*

⁴⁴*"Our ancestors had the tabernacle of the covenant law with them in the wilderness. It had been made as God directed Moses, according to the pattern he had seen. ⁴⁵After receiving the tabernacle, our ancestors under Joshua brought it with them when they took the land from the nations God drove out before them. It remained in the land until the time of David, ⁴⁶who enjoyed God's favor and asked that he might provide a dwelling*

place for the God of Jacob. ⁴⁷But it was Solomon who built a house for him.

⁴⁸"However, the Most High does not live in houses made by human hands. As the prophet says: ⁴⁹"'Heaven is my throne, and the earth is my footstool. What kind of house will you build for me? says the Lord. Or where will my resting place be? ⁵⁰Has not my hand made all these things?'

⁵¹"You stiff-necked people! Your hearts and ears are still uncircumcised. You are just like your ancestors: You always resist the Holy Spirit! ⁵²Was there ever a prophet your ancestors did not persecute? They even killed those who predicted the coming of the Righteous One. And now you have betrayed and murdered him— ⁵³you who have received the law that was given through angels but have not obeyed it."

⁵⁴When the members of the Sanhedrin heard this, they were furious and gnashed their teeth at him. ⁵⁵But Stephen, full of the Holy Spirit, looked up to heaven and saw the glory of God, and Jesus standing at the right hand of God. ⁵⁶"Look," he said, "I see heaven open and the Son of Man standing at the right hand of God."

⁵⁷At this they covered their ears and, yelling at the top of their voices, they all rushed at him, ⁵⁸dragged him out of the city and began to stone him. Meanwhile, the witnesses laid their coats at the feet of a young man named Saul.

⁵⁹While they were stoning him, Stephen prayed, "Lord Jesus,

receive my spirit." ⁶⁰*Then he fell on his knees and cried out, "Lord, do not hold this sin against them." When he had said this, he fell asleep.*

REFLECTION

In every great adventure, the hero and villain have back-stories that slowly unfold through the movie. Their back-stories explain their actions, the source of their conflict and the problems that have increased the hostility between them. Their conflict moves toward a climactic battle which decides the future for all those involved.

Stephen, as a devout Hebrew, had memorized the story of Israel and recited it that day to the religious leaders. Their origin was in Abraham; their identity in Jacob; their deliverance from Egyptian slavery had come through Moses and their entrance into the Promised Land had come through Joshua.

Stephen didn't stop there though: he also shared the ugly back-story that went through that history. It was not one of devotion and faithfulness to God: just the opposite. The Jewish people had always been "stiff-necked" and resistant to the Holy Spirit. And now, their resistance and hostility to God had led to the climactic moment of the Bible: the crucifixion of their Messiah, Jesus. That climax revealed that they were villains, not good guys.

This is not the story the Jewish leaders wanted to see or hear. They thought of themselves as the heroes, the good guys, but the murders of Jesus *and* Stephen revealed that they were truly bad guys (as we all are in our sin!). God had continued to bless them throughout their history purely out of His graciousness. They had done nothing to deserve it. And it is God alone, specially revealed in Jesus Christ, who is the true hero of the Bible.

Jesus' life, from his conception to his resurrection, is the climatic turning point, not just of the Bible but of history. His death and resurrection addressed the deepest problems of sin, which affected the Jewish people as much as the Gentiles they looked down on. It is only as we accept that we are all "bad guys" in need of a Savior that we will find our happy ending and true, ultimate hero in Jesus Christ.

CORRELATION

What shall we conclude then? Are we [Jews] any better? Not at all! We have already made the charge that Jews and Gentiles alike are all under sin.

Romans 3:9

The high priest said to him, "I charge you under oath by the living God: Tell us if you are the Messiah, the Son of God." "You have said so," Jesus replied. "But I say to all of you: From now on you will see the Son of Man sitting at the right hand of the Mighty One and coming on the clouds of heaven." Then the high priest tore his clothes and said, "He has spoken blasphemy! Why do we need any more witnesses? Look, now you have heard the blasphemy.

Matthew 26:63-65

RECITATION

Lord Jesus Christ, Son of God, have mercy on me, a sinner.

The Jesus Prayer

> Recite three times slowly.

APPLICATION

> What has come to mind, either through the passage or in your reflection that you want to remember?

Sharing the Word

Passage: Acts 8:26-40

Meditation: Acts 8:26-40
Pause and Reflect Silently
Highlight Key Phrases
Look to and Lift up Christ

²⁶*Now an angel of the Lord said to Philip, "Go south to the road—the desert road—that goes down from Jerusalem to Gaza." ²⁷So he started out, and on his way he met an Ethiopian eunuch, an important official in charge of all the treasury of the Kandake (which means "queen of the Ethiopians").*

This man had gone to Jerusalem to worship, ²⁸and on his way home was sitting in his chariot reading the Book of Isaiah the prophet. ²⁹The Spirit told Philip, "Go to that chariot and stay near it."

³⁰*Then Philip ran up to the chariot and heard the man reading Isaiah the prophet. "Do you understand what you are reading?" Philip asked.*

³¹*"How can I," he said, "unless someone explains it to me?" So he invited Philip to come up and sit with him.*

³²*This is the passage of Scripture the eunuch was reading:*

> "He was led like a sheep to the slaughter,
>   and as a lamb before its shearer is silent,
>   so he did not open his mouth.
> ³³In his humiliation he was deprived of justice.
>   Who can speak of his descendants?
>   For his life was taken from the earth."

³⁴The eunuch asked Philip, "Tell me, please, who is the prophet talking about, himself or someone else?" ³⁵Then Philip began with that very passage of Scripture and told him the good news about Jesus.

³⁶As they traveled along the road, they came to some water and the eunuch said, "Look, here is water. What can stand in the way of my being baptized?" ³⁸And he gave orders to stop the chariot. Then both Philip and the eunuch went down into the water and Philip baptized him.

³⁹When they came up out of the water, the Spirit of the Lord suddenly took Philip away, and the eunuch did not see him again, but went on his way rejoicing. ⁴⁰Philip, however, appeared at Azotus and traveled about, preaching the gospel in all the towns until he reached Caesarea.

REFLECTION

When Jesus commissioned his followers he told them that they would be his witnesses to 1) Jerusalem, 2) Judea and Samaria and 3) the ends of the earth (1:8). This encounter in Philip's ministry shows how his first followers began entering into what for them was "the ends of the earth."

Philip was one of the first deacons with Stephen (Acts 6:5). God used him to expand the church's witness into Samaria (Acts 8) and then into northern Africa through this Ethiopian official, who was a non-Jew who had converted to Judaism.

There were different "levels" of conversion in Judaism. Some became proselytes who fully embraced Judaism through circumcision and acceptance of its social, dietary, and ritual laws, while others became "near converts" who were called "God-fearers" who embraced monotheism and its morality but did not fully embrace Judaism's lifestyle laws.

We are not told what type of convert this man was but we are told that he was a eunuch, someone who either voluntarily or involuntarily had been emasculated (I'll let you look that up!). Interestingly enough the prophet Isaiah had a special promise for those who were eunuchs (Is 56:3-8) and this might have led this official to buy a copy of Isaiah to bring back with him.

The official "just happened" to be reading Isaiah 53, one of the most detailed prophecies of Jesus' death in the Bible, as Philip approached him. And Philip "just happened" to know the fuller meaning of Isaiah's prophesy. God's presence and work in our lives is often experienced through these amazingly orchestrated "coincidences."

The Ethiopian's excitement led him to seek baptism. Christian baptism went beyond the baptism of John, which focused on repentance from sin, to become a public identification with Jesus in his life, death and resurrection. Each convert would in essence be testifying, "I have been spiritually buried and have risen again with Christ."

CORRELATION

We were therefore buried with him through baptism into death in order that, just as Christ was raised from the dead through the glory of the Father, we too may live a new life.
Romans 3:4

Let us draw near to God with a sincere heart and with the full assurance that faith brings, having our hearts sprinkled to cleanse us from a guilty conscience and having our bodies washed with pure water.
Hebrews 10:22

RECITATION

I believe in God the Father, Almighty Maker of heaven and earth.

And in Jesus Christ his only Son our Lord; who was conceived by the Holy Spirit,

born of the Virgin Mary, suffered under Pontius Pilate, was crucified, dead, and buried; he descended into hell; the third day he rose again from the dead;

He ascended into heaven, and sits on the right hand of God the Father Almighty; from there he shall come to judge the living and the dead.

I believe in the Holy Spirit; the holy Christian Church; the communion of saints; the forgiveness of sins; the resurrection of the body; and the life everlasting. AMEN.

The Apostle's Creed

APPLICATION

What has come to mind, either through the passage or in your reflection that you want to remember?

Good News For All

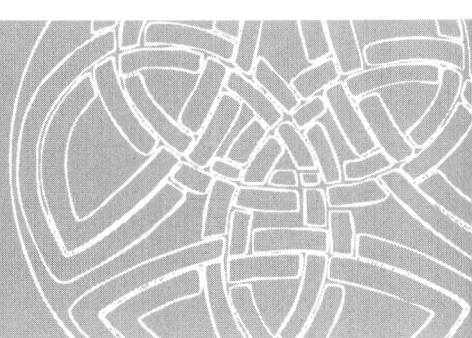

Passage: Acts 10:1-11:18

Meditation: Acts 10:25-46
Pause and Reflect Silently
Highlight Key Phrases
Look to and Lift up Christ

²⁵*As Peter entered the house, Cornelius met him and fell at his feet in reverence.* ²⁶*But Peter made him get up. "Stand up," he said, "I am only a man myself."* ²⁷*While talking with him, Peter went inside and found a large gathering of people.* ²⁸*He said to them: "You are well aware that it is against our law for a Jew to associate with or visit a Gentile. But God has shown me that I should not call anyone impure or unclean.* ²⁹*So when I was sent for, I came without raising any objection. May I ask why you sent for me?"*

³⁰*Cornelius answered: "Three days ago I was in my house praying at this hour, at three in the afternoon. Suddenly a man in shining clothes stood before me* ³¹*and said, 'Cornelius, God has heard your prayer and remembered your gifts to the poor.* ³²*Send to Joppa for Simon who is called Peter. He is a guest in the home of Simon the tanner, who lives by the sea.'* ³³*So I sent for you immediately, and it was good of you to come. Now we*

are all here in the presence of God to listen to everything the Lord has commanded you to tell us."

³⁴Then Peter began to speak: "I now realize how true it is that God does not show favoritism ³⁵but accepts from every nation the one who fears him and does what is right. ³⁶You know the message God sent to the people of Israel, announcing the good news of peace through Jesus Christ, who is Lord of all. ³⁷You know what has happened throughout the province of Judea, beginning in Galilee after the baptism that John preached— ³⁸how God anointed Jesus of Nazareth with the Holy Spirit and power, and how he went around doing good and healing all who were under the power of the devil, because God was with him.

³⁹"We are witnesses of everything he did in the country of the Jews and in Jerusalem. They killed him by hanging him on a cross, ⁴⁰but God raised him from the dead on the third day and caused him to be seen. ⁴¹He was not seen by all the people, but by witnesses whom God had already chosen—by us who ate and drank with him after he rose from the dead. ⁴²He commanded us to preach to the people and to testify that he is the one whom God appointed as judge of the living and the dead. ⁴³All the prophets testify about him that everyone who believes in him receives forgiveness of sins through his name."

⁴⁴While Peter was still speaking these words, the Holy Spirit came on all who heard the message. ⁴⁵The circumcised believers who had come with Peter were astonished that the gift of the

Holy Spirit had been poured out even on Gentiles. ⁴⁶For they heard them speaking in tongues and praising God.

REFLECTION

The big question in the Church's earliest days was, "Did a Christian have to live under the Mosaic Law to be in good-standing with God?" The story of Cornelius continues the process of clarifying the answer to that question.

Going back to Moses' time, God's people had been defined as Jacob's descendants who had agreed to the covenant obligations of living under the Law given at Mt Sinai. God had also made provisions for non-Jews to join His people and those commands had guided the Jewish people for centuries.

Jewish Christians believed that those guidelines were still in force. They believed that Christian converts still needed to live under the Mosaic Law's social, dietary and ritual commands. They believed to do otherwise was a violation of their covenant agreement with God. In their minds they had both Scripture and tradition on their side.

We cannot over-estimate how radical and uncomfortable it was for devout Jewish believers to consider the possibility that you could be in good-standing with God and "ignore" the Law. It seemed sacrilegious. Before they could even contemplate the idea they would need dramatic proof of divine approval. And that approval would need to be communicated through someone they looked up to and trusted.

The Apostle Peter fulfilled that role. God gave him a vision *three times* to convince him of the radical changes He was instituting in His relationship with His people. Cornelius and his family's reception of the Holy Spirit, with the same sign of tongues that the Jewish believers had received on Pentecost, convinced Peter and the Jewish Christians with him that God was confirming their freedom from the demands of the Mosaic Law. All of these supernatural signs were needed to begin the process of acceptance among those Jewish believers. Unfortunately, in spite of all this, many never could.

CORRELATION

You foolish Galatians! Who has bewitched you? Before your very eyes Jesus Christ was clearly portrayed as crucified. I would like to learn just one thing from you: Did you receive the Spirit by the works of the law, or by believing what you heard?

Galatians 3:1-2

Before the coming of this faith, we were held in custody under the law, locked up until the faith that was to come would be revealed. So the law was our guardian until Christ came that we might be justified by faith.

Galatians 3:23-24

RECITATION

O Father, light up
    the small duties of this day's life;

May they shine
    with the beauty of Your countenance.

May we believe that glory can dwell
    in the commonest task of every day.

Augustine of Hippo

APPLICATION

What has come to mind, either through the passage or in your reflection that you want to remember?

The Road To Damascus

Passage: Acts 9:1-31

Meditation: Acts 9:1-22
Pause and Reflect Silently
Highlight Key Phrases
Look to and Lift up Christ

¹*Meanwhile, Saul was still breathing out murderous threats against the Lord's disciples. He went to the high priest* ²*and asked him for letters to the synagogues in Damascus, so that if he found any there who belonged to the Way, whether men or women, he might take them as prisoners to Jerusalem.*

³*As he neared Damascus on his journey, suddenly a light from heaven flashed around him.* ⁴*He fell to the ground and heard a voice say to him, "Saul, Saul, why do you persecute me?"* ⁵*"Who are you, Lord?" Saul asked. "I am Jesus, whom you are persecuting," he replied.* ⁶*"Now get up and go into the city, and you will be told what you must do."*

⁷*The men traveling with Saul stood there speechless; they heard the sound but did not see anyone.* ⁸*Saul got up from the ground, but when he opened his eyes he could see nothing. So they led him by the hand into Damascus.* ⁹*For three days he was blind, and did not eat or drink anything.*

¹⁰*In Damascus there was a disciple named Ananias. The Lord*

called to him in a vision, "Ananias!" "Yes, Lord," he answered. ¹¹The Lord told him, "Go to the house of Judas on Straight Street and ask for a man from Tarsus named Saul, for he is praying. ¹²In a vision he has seen a man named Ananias come and place his hands on him to restore his sight."

¹³"Lord," Ananias answered, "I have heard many reports about this man and all the harm he has done to your holy people in Jerusalem. ¹⁴And he has come here with authority from the chief priests to arrest all who call on your name." ¹⁵But the Lord said to Ananias, "Go! This man is my chosen instrument to proclaim my name to the Gentiles and their kings and to the people of Israel. ¹⁶I will show him how much he must suffer for my name."

¹⁷Then Ananias went to the house and entered it. Placing his hands on Saul, he said, "Brother Saul, the Lord—Jesus, who appeared to you on the road as you were coming here—has sent me so that you may see again and be filled with the Holy Spirit."

¹⁸Immediately, something like scales fell from Saul's eyes, and he could see again. He got up and was baptized, ¹⁹and after taking some food, he regained his strength. Saul spent several days with the disciples in Damascus. ²⁰At once he began to preach in the synagogues that Jesus is the Son of God. ²¹All those who heard him were astonished and asked, "Isn't he the man who raised havoc in Jerusalem among those who call on this name? And hasn't he come here to take them as prisoners to the chief priests?" ²²Yet Saul grew more and more powerful and baffled the Jews living in Damascus by proving that Jesus is the Messiah.

REFLECTION

The list of proofs for Jesus' resurrection begins with his earliest followers, whose radical transformations need an even more radical event to explain them. Another proof at the top of the list is the conversion of Saul of Tarsus.

Saul is the *"last person"* you would have expected to preach Christ. His conversion was so significant that Acts describes the moment in detail and records Saul, later named Paul, explaining its importance two more times (Acts 22,26). Unfortunately, the closest parallels to Saul are found in today's Islamic Jihadists. He, like them, was a fanatic who was convinced of his religious superiority and found nothing wrong with taking the lives of people who offended his religion.

Saul was divinely struck blind one day on the road to the Syrian city of Damascus. He had been spiritually blind to the reality of who he was fighting against: the very God he professed to follow.

Saul was named after the first king of Israel and the contrast between their two lives is significant: Saul the king experienced God's rejection because of his sin (1 Sam 15) and spent the rest of his life fighting against the Lord's anointed, David. Saul the convert experienced God's redemption from his sin and spent the rest of his life fighting for the Lord's Anointed, Jesus!

Conversion experiences are often followed by a long period of re-evaluation in belief systems, morality and world-view. Saul spent three days in visual darkness, quickly coming to grips with the new spiritual light he had been given by God. His response is instructive.

When the "scales" fell away he did what we are all called to do: 1) believe in Christ; 2) be baptized by water; 3) connect with other Christians and 4) share what we have learned with others. Thank God, too, for Ananias, who had enough courage to trust God and become the first bridge for Saul into the Christian community.

CORRELATION

> *[The Jailer] brought them out and asked, "Sirs, what must I do to be saved?" They replied, "Believe in the Lord Jesus, and you will be saved--you and your household."* Acts 16:30-31

RECITATION

LORD, MAKE ME AN INSTRUMENT OF YOUR PEACE,

where there is hatred, let me sow love,

where there is injury, pardon,

where there is discord, may I bring harmony,

where there is error, may I bring truth,

where there is doubt, may I bring faith,

where there is despair, may I bring hope,

where there is darkness, may I bring light,

and where there is sadness, may I bring joy.

O Divine Master,

grant that I may not so much seek

to be consoled, as to console,

to be understood, as to understand,

to be loved, as to love.

for it is in giving that we receive;

it is in pardoning that we are pardoned;

and it is in dying that we are born into eternal life.

Francis of Assisi

APPLICATION

What has come to mind, either through the passage or in your reflection that you want to remember?

The First Missionary Journey

Passage: Acts 13:1-14:28

Meditation: Acts 14:1-20
Pause and Reflect Silently
Highlight Key Phrases
Look to and Lift up Christ

¹At Iconium Paul and Barnabas went as usual into the Jewish synagogue. There they spoke so effectively that a great number of Jews and Greeks believed.

²But the Jews who refused to believe stirred up the other Gentiles and poisoned their minds against the brothers. ³So Paul and Barnabas spent considerable time there, speaking boldly for the Lord, who confirmed the message of his grace by enabling them to perform signs and wonders.

⁴The people of the city were divided; some sided with the Jews, others with the apostles. ⁵There was a plot afoot among both Gentiles and Jews, together with their leaders, to mistreat them and stone them. ⁶But they found out about it and fled to the Lycaonian cities of Lystra and Derbe and to the surrounding country, ⁷where they continued to preach the gospel.

⁸In Lystra there sat a man who was lame. He had been that way from birth and had never walked. ⁹He listened to Paul as he

was speaking. Paul looked directly at him, saw that he had faith to be healed [10]and called out, "Stand up on your feet!" At that, the man jumped up and began to walk.

[11]When the crowd saw what Paul had done, they shouted in the Lycaonian language, "The gods have come down to us in human form!" [12]Barnabas they called Zeus, and Paul they called Hermes because he was the chief speaker. [13]The priest of Zeus, whose temple was just outside the city, brought bulls and wreaths to the city gates because he and the crowd wanted to offer sacrifices to them.

[14]But when the apostles Barnabas and Paul heard of this, they tore their clothes and rushed out into the crowd, shouting: [15]"Friends, why are you doing this? We too are only human, like you. We are bringing you good news, telling you to turn from these worthless things to the living God, who made the heavens and the earth and the sea and everything in them. [16]In the past, he let all nations go their own way. [17]Yet he has not left himself without testimony: He has shown kindness by giving you rain from heaven and crops in their seasons; he provides you with plenty of food and fills your hearts with joy." [18]Even with these words, they had difficulty keeping the crowd from sacrificing to them.

[19]Then some Jews came from Antioch and Iconium and won the crowd over. They stoned Paul and dragged him outside the city, thinking he was dead. [20]But after the disciples had gathered around him, he got up and went back into the city. The next day he and Barnabas left for Derbe.

REFLECTION

Jerusalem was the first city of Christianity. It was the center of the Christian movement for the first few decades after Jesus' resurrection. Antioch became the second key city in the Christian movement and the church there had the privilege of sending the first missionaries "overseas."

Before Jesus ascended to heaven, he told his followers to wait on the gift of the Holy Spirit. Their waiting led them up to Pentecost when the Holy Spirit descended on them in a spectacular way (Acts 2). The church in Antioch had a similar but unique experience: they were waiting on the Lord in worship when the Spirit spoke to them about commissioning Barnabas and Paul as the first missionaries. Notice that these capable leaders were submissive to both the church and the Spirit.

Barnabas was from the island of Cyprus, and thus the first missionary journey began among the Jewish population where he grew up. There were large numbers of Jewish people throughout the Roman Empire. They were part of what was called the Diaspora, or a dispersion of people from their homeland. The Jewish people who lived in foreign countries became the strongest opponents of the Apostle Paul and the early Christian movement.

The first missionary journey continued into Asia Minor, or what we call Southern Turkey today. Paul's letter to the Galatians was probably written to the churches they visited in that area. Barnabas and Paul experienced the full gamut of responses on their journey: at one point the people thought they were gods, while at another Paul was stoned and left for dead (you wonder if he thought much about the martyr Stephen as he lay there). Through it all, people responded to the message about Christ and the first churches of Asia Minor were begun.

CORRELATION

I came to you in weakness with great fear and trembling. My message and my preaching were not with wise and persuasive words, but with a demonstration of the Spirit's power, so that your faith might not rest on human wisdom, but on God's power.

1 Corinthians 2:3-5

It is for freedom that Christ has set us free. Stand firm, then, and do not let yourselves be burdened again by a yoke of slavery.

Galatians 5:13

RECITATION

Thanks be to you, our Lord Jesus Christ,

For all the benefits you have given us,

For all the pains and insults you have borne for us.

Most merciful Redeemer, Friend, and Brother,

May we know you more clearly,

Love you more dearly,

And follow you more nearly:

Forever and ever. AMEN.

Richard Chichester

APPLICATION

What has come to mind, either through the passage or in your reflection that you want to remember?

The Council at Jerusalem

Passage: Acts 15:1-41

Meditation: Acts 15:1-20
Pause and Reflect Silently
Highlight Key Phrases
Look to and Lift up Christ

¹*Certain people came down from Judea to Antioch and were teaching the believers: "Unless you are circumcised, according to the custom taught by Moses, you cannot be saved."*

²*This brought Paul and Barnabas into sharp dispute and debate with them. So Paul and Barnabas were appointed, along with some other believers, to go up to Jerusalem to see the apostles and elders about this question.*

³*The church sent them on their way, and as they traveled through Phoenicia and Samaria, they told how the Gentiles had been converted. This news made all the believers very glad.* ⁴*When they came to Jerusalem, they were welcomed by the church and the apostles and elders, to whom they reported everything God had done through them.*

⁵*Then some of the believers who belonged to the party of the Pharisees stood up and said, "The Gentiles must be circumcised*

and required to keep the law of Moses." ⁶The apostles and elders met to consider this question.

⁷After much discussion, Peter got up and addressed them: "Brothers, you know that some time ago God made a choice among you that the Gentiles might hear from my lips the message of the gospel and believe. ⁸God, who knows the heart, showed that he accepted them by giving the Holy Spirit to them, just as he did to us. ⁹He did not discriminate between us and them, for he purified their hearts by faith. ¹⁰Now then, why do you try to test God by putting on the necks of Gentiles a yoke that neither we nor our ancestors have been able to bear? ¹¹No! We believe it is through the grace of our Lord Jesus that we are saved, just as they are."

¹²The whole assembly became silent as they listened to Barnabas and Paul telling about the signs and wonders God had done among the Gentiles through them. ¹³When they finished, James spoke up. "Brothers," he said, "listen to me. ¹⁴ Simon has described to us how God first intervened to choose a people for his name from the Gentiles. ¹⁵The words of the prophets are in agreement with this, as it is written: ¹⁶"'After this I will return and rebuild David's fallen tent. Its ruins I will rebuild, and I will restore it, ¹⁷that the rest of mankind may seek the Lord, even all the Gentiles who bear my name, says the Lord, who does these things'—¹⁸things known from long ago. ¹⁹"It is my judgment, therefore, that we should not make it difficult for the Gentiles who are turning to God. ²⁰Instead we should write to them, telling them to abstain from food polluted by idols, from sexual immorality, from the meat of strangled animals and from blood.

REFLECTION

The first convened council in Christian history dealt with the central issue of their time: did a Gentile believer need to become Jewish in their observance of the Law of Moses? The early Jewish Christians believed Jesus to be the Messiah, or Anointed One of God, and generally understood that it was their faith in him that brought them into a right relationship with God. But how do you maintain that belief and right relationship? For many of them there was no question: you honor the social, dietary and ritual Laws of Moses. If you did not honor these laws you were a sinner and dishonored God. Case Closed.

Acts 15 shows how the most significant leaders in the church all agreed that this was no longer the case. Jews could still chose to live under the Mosaic Law but Gentiles had no obligation to do so. Peter, Barnabas, Paul and then James all support this interpretation. It was a monumental moment: true human freedom from religious obligation was unknown in the ancient world. Christianity proclaimed that God was finished with animal sacrifices and no longer demanded obedience to the Law of Moses to become a part of His forever family. Christianity is about keeping the main thing the main thing: loving God and loving others just as Jesus would.

The final word of the Council to Gentile believers was for them to respect the convictions of Jewish believers and not give in to sexual immorality (fornication). Unfortunately, the harmonious Council was followed by a painful split between Barnabas and Paul: both had strong convictions, neither sinned specifically, and yet they ended up parting ways in their mission work. What can we learn from this? Many things of course, but we should celebrate the moments of harmony and trust God with the moments when things do not go the way we expect or hope for.

CORRELATION

For in Christ Jesus neither circumcision nor un-circumcision has any value. The only thing that counts is faith expressing itself through love. Galatians 5:6

RECITATION

Lord, whatever this day may bring

Your name be praised.

Be gracious to me and help me.

Grant me strength to bear whatever you may send,
   and let not fear overrule me.

I trust your grace and commit my life wholly into your
   hands.

Whether I live or whether I die, I am with you.

And you are with me,

O my Lord and my God.

Lord, I wait for your salvation,
   and for the coming of your kingdom. AMEN.

Dietrich Bonhoeffer

APPLICATION

What has come to mind, either through the passage or in your reflection that you want to remember?

Missionary Journeys

Passage: Acts 16:1-17:34

Meditation: Acts 16:11-31
Pause and Reflect Silently
Highlight Key Phrases
Look to and Lift up Christ

[11]From Troas we put out to sea and sailed straight for Samothrace, and the next day we went on to Neapolis. [12]From there we traveled to Philippi, a Roman colony and the leading city of that district of Macedonia. And we stayed there several days. [13]On the Sabbath we went outside the city gate to the river, where we expected to find a place of prayer. We sat down and began to speak to the women who had gathered there.

[14]One of those listening was a woman from the city of Thyatira named Lydia, a dealer in purple cloth. She was a worshiper of God. The Lord opened her heart to respond to Paul's message. [15]When she and the members of her household were baptized, she invited us to her home. "If you consider me a believer in the Lord," she said, "come and stay at my house." And she persuaded us.

[16]Once when we were going to the place of prayer, we were met by a female slave who had a spirit by which she predicted the

future. She earned a great deal of money for her owners by fortune-telling. [17] She followed Paul and the rest of us, shouting, "These men are servants of the Most High God, who are telling you the way to be saved." [18] She kept this up for many days. Finally Paul became so annoyed that he turned around and said to the spirit, "In the name of Jesus Christ I command you to come out of her!" At that moment the spirit left her.

[19] When her owners realized that their hope of making money was gone, they seized Paul and Silas and dragged them into the marketplace to face the authorities. [20] They brought them before the magistrates and said, "These men are Jews, and are throwing our city into an uproar [21] by advocating customs unlawful for us Romans to accept or practice." [22] The crowd joined in the attack against Paul and Silas, and the magistrates ordered them to be stripped and beaten with rods. [23] After they had been severely flogged, they were thrown into prison, and the jailer was commanded to guard them carefully. [24] When he received these orders, he put them in the inner cell and fastened their feet in the stocks.

[25] About midnight Paul and Silas were praying and singing hymns to God, and the other prisoners were listening to them. [26] Suddenly there was such a violent earthquake that the foundations of the prison were shaken. At once all the prison doors flew open, and everyone's chains came loose. [27] The jailer woke up, and when he saw the prison doors open, he drew his sword and was about to kill himself because he thought the prisoners had escaped. [28] But Paul shouted, "Don't harm yourself! We are all here!"

²⁹The jailer called for lights, rushed in and fell trembling before Paul and Silas. ³⁰He then brought them out and asked, "Sirs, what must I do to be saved?" ³¹They replied, "Believe in the Lord Jesus, and you will be saved—you and your household."

REFLECTION

The Apostle Paul's journeys are usually broken down into four. The first began on the island of Cyprus and centered on Southern Turkey. The second began in Central Turkey and brought the Christian movement into Europe for the first recorded time (Acts 16-18). The third was a "return trip" to places he visited on his second journey; it mostly centered on his ministry in Ephesus, and ended in Jerusalem (Acts 19-23). The fourth journey was taken as a prisoner, as Paul was shipped to Rome to stand trial before Caesar for charges filed against him by the Jewish authorities (Acts 24-28). Our reading focuses on Paul's second journey and introduces us to those who became Paul's closest ministry partners: the Philippian Christians.

Paul's adventures would have read like a spiritual Indiana Jones story. It would have given those early believers a bigger picture of what they were a part of. Christianity was the first trans-cultural religious movement in history. Up to that point, people followed their own cultural religious practices. A pious person was someone who honored the gods of their people. The Romans generally respected and encouraged the people's religious practices.

But the early Christians confused everyone: they renounced their traditional gods and called for people to give allegiance to a Jewish prophet who had died a humiliating death on a cross. Roman authorities actually considered Christians atheists because of their rejection of their ancestral gods. Thus the early Christians found themselves rejecting much of their own cultural heritage, being misunderstood by the Roman authorities, and persecuted by Jewish people for a Jewish man they had never met. Paul's adventures would have given them the understanding and assurances they needed to face the social isolation and, at times, persecution they all experienced.

CORRELATION

One night the Lord spoke to Paul in a vision: "Do not be afraid; keep on speaking, do not be silent. For I am with you, and no one is going to attack and harm you, because I have many people in this city." Acts 18:9-10

RECITATION

GOD, GRANT ME THE SERENITY
to accept the things I cannot change;

Courage to change the things I can and
the wisdom to know the difference.

To live one day at a time;
enjoying one moment at a time;

Accepting hardship as the pathway to peace.

To take, as He did, this sinful world as it is, not as I would have it.

Trusting that He will make all things right if I surrender to His Will.

That I may be reasonably happy in this life and supremely happy with You forever in the next. AMEN.

Reinhold Neibuhr

APPLICATION

What has come to mind, either through the passage or in your reflection that you want to remember?

The Trial Before Festus

Passage: Acts 25:1-26:32

Meditation: Acts 26:2-20
Pause and Reflect Silently
Highlight Key Phrases
Look to and Lift up Christ

²*"King Agrippa, I consider myself fortunate to stand before you today as I make my defense against all the accusations of the Jews, ³and especially so because you are well acquainted with all the Jewish customs and controversies. Therefore, I beg you to listen to me patiently.*

⁴*"The Jewish people all know the way I have lived ever since I was a child, from the beginning of my life in my own country, and also in Jerusalem. ⁵They have known me for a long time and can testify, if they are willing, that I conformed to the strictest sect of our religion, living as a Pharisee.*

⁶*And now it is because of my hope in what God has promised our ancestors that I am on trial today. ⁷This is the promise our twelve tribes are hoping to see fulfilled as they earnestly serve God day and night. King Agrippa, it is because of this hope that these Jews are accusing me. ⁸Why should any of you consider it incredible that God raises the dead?*

⁹"I too was convinced that I ought to do all that was possible to oppose the name of Jesus of Nazareth. ¹⁰And that is just what I did in Jerusalem. On the authority of the chief priests I put many of the Lord's people in prison, and when they were put to death, I cast my vote against them. ¹¹Many a time I went from one synagogue to another to have them punished, and I tried to force them to blaspheme. I was so obsessed with persecuting them that I even hunted them down in foreign cities.

¹²"On one of these journeys I was going to Damascus with the authority and commission of the chief priests. ¹³About noon, King Agrippa, as I was on the road, I saw a light from heaven, brighter than the sun, blazing around me and my companions. ¹⁴We all fell to the ground, and I heard a voice saying to me in Aramaic, 'Saul, Saul, why do you persecute me? It is hard for you to kick against the goads.' ¹⁵"Then I asked, 'Who are you, Lord?'

"'I am Jesus, whom you are persecuting,' the Lord replied. ¹⁶'Now get up and stand on your feet. I have appeared to you to appoint you as a servant and as a witness of what you have seen and will see of me. ¹⁷I will rescue you from your own people and from the Gentiles. I am sending you to them ¹⁸to open their eyes and turn them from darkness to light, and from the power of Satan to God, so that they may receive forgiveness of sins and a place among those who are sanctified by faith in me.'

¹⁹"So then, King Agrippa, I was not disobedient to the vision from heaven. ²⁰First to those in Damascus, then to those in Je-

rusalem and in all Judea, and then to the Gentiles, I preached that they should repent and turn to God and demonstrate their repentance by their deeds.

REFLECTION

The Gospel of Luke and the Book of Acts both have a similar outline. A new movement of God is begun through a forerunner (John the Baptist, Peter) and advances through God's appointed leader (Jesus, Paul). Both end with court trials. Jesus was tried before the Jewish Sanhedrin and the Roman leader, Pontius Pilate. Paul was "tried" before the Sanhedrin and two Roman governors: Felix and Festus. Both trials highlight the evil intentions of the Jewish leaders of the time.

Festus began his rule over Judea around 59 AD and died about two years later. The Jewish leaders tried to take advantage of his inexperience but he maintained control by ensuring that Paul's trial took place outside of Judea in the coastal city of Caesarea. At the end of his trial, Paul claimed his right as a Roman citizen to appeal to Caesar. Roman law during this period allowed a citizen to appeal their case before the imperial court, if the person faced the threat of violence and coercion by local leaders. They could appeal to the higher court and the local governors were obligated to agree.

Paul's trial was followed with an audience before King Agrippa, who was the great-grandson of Herod the Great, who ruled Judea when Jesus was born. Paul goes into detail about his conversion experience with Christ and how he was commissioned by Him to "open their eyes and turn them from darkness to light, and from the power of Satan to God."

When we think of Paul's ministry we may not realize how much of it he spent in prison. He probably spent five and one-half to six years of his ministry career in prison. Of the thirteen letters we have written by him, five were written from a prison. Paul spent more than two years in prison in Caesarea, yet it was during this time that Luke probably interviewed the people who helped him write his gospel and this book of Acts.

CORRELATION

Many have undertaken to draw up an account of the things that have been fulfilled among us... I myself have carefully investigated everything from the beginning... so that you may know the certainty of the things you have been taught.

Excerpted from **Luke 1:1-4**

RECITATION

Father, we give you thanks for all the gifts you freely bestow on us. For the beauty and wonder of your creation, in earth and sky and sea, Lord, we thank you.

For our daily food and drink, our homes and families, and our friends, Lord, we thank you.

For minds to think, and hearts to love, and hands to serve, Lord, we thank you. For health and strength to work, and leisure to rest and play, Lord, we thank you.

For the brave and courageous, who are patient in suffering and faithful in adversity, Lord, we thank you.

For the communion of saints, in all times and places, Lord, we thank you.

Above all, we give you thanks for the great mercies and promises given to us in Christ Jesus our Lord; to him be praise and glory, with you, O Father, and the Holy Spirit, now and forever. AMEN.

APPLICATION

What has come to mind, either through the passage or in your reflection that you want to remember?

More Than Conquerors

Passage: Romans 8:1-38

Meditation: Romans 8:18-34
Pause and Reflect Silently
Highlight Key Phrases
Look to and Lift up Christ

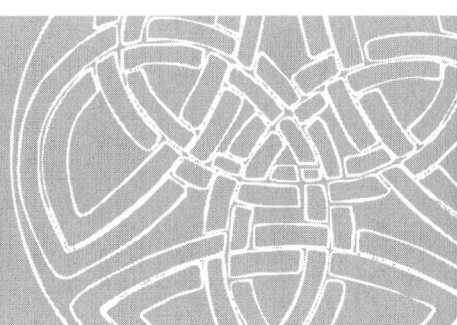

¹⁸*I consider that our present sufferings are not worth comparing with the glory that will be revealed in us.* ¹⁹*For the creation waits in eager expectation for the children of God to be revealed.*

²⁰*For the creation was subjected to frustration, not by its own choice, but by the will of the one who subjected it, in hope* ²¹*that the creation itself will be liberated from its bondage to decay and brought into the freedom and glory of the children of God.*

²²*We know that the whole creation has been groaning as in the pains of childbirth right up to the present time.* ²³*Not only so, but we ourselves, who have the firstfruits of the Spirit, groan inwardly as we wait eagerly for our adoption to sonship, the redemption of our bodies.* ²⁴*For in this hope we were saved.*

But hope that is seen is no hope at all. Who hopes for what they already have? ²⁵*But if we hope for what we do not yet have, we wait for it patiently.*

²⁶In the same way, the Spirit helps us in our weakness. We do not know what we ought to pray for, but the Spirit himself intercedes for us through wordless groans. ²⁷And he who searches our hearts knows the mind of the Spirit, because the Spirit intercedes for God's people in accordance with the will of God.

²⁸And we know that in all things God works for the good of those who love him, who have been called according to his purpose. ²⁹For those God foreknew he also predestined to be conformed to the image of his Son, that he might be the firstborn among many brothers and sisters. ³⁰And those he predestined, he also called; those he called, he also justified; those he justified, he also glorified.

³¹What, then, shall we say in response to these things? If God is for us, who can be against us? ³²He who did not spare his own Son, but gave him up for us all—how will he not also, along with him, graciously give us all things? ³³Who will bring any charge against those whom God has chosen? It is God who justifies. ³⁴Who then is the one who condemns? No one. Christ Jesus who died—more than that, who was raised to life—is at the right hand of God and is also interceding for us.

³⁵Who shall separate us from the love of Christ? Shall trouble or hardship or persecution or famine or nakedness or danger or sword? ³⁶As it is written: "For your sake we face death all day long; we are considered as sheep to be slaughtered." ³⁷No, in all these things we are more than conquerors through him who loved us. ³⁸For I am convinced that neither death nor life,

neither angels nor demons, neither the present nor the future, nor any powers, ³⁹neither height nor depth, nor anything else in all creation, will be able to separate us from the love of God that is in Christ Jesus our Lord.

REFLECTION

Romans 8 is one of the pinnacles of the New Testament. In it, Paul explains the glorious blessings that Christians enter into when they receive Christ. Paul's focus in Romans is on the Gospel and the righteousness of God (1:14-17).

The *Gospel* is the Good News of what God has done for mankind through the person and work of Jesus Christ (and all the implications that come with them). The *righteousness of God* is understood in two different ways. Either it is seen as 1) God's faithfulness in fulfilling His Old Testament promises, especially those given to Abraham or as 2) Christ's faithfulness in perfectly living up to God's intentions in the Law of Moses. Both concepts are present in Romans. Either way, Paul wants us to understand and celebrate the glories of the righteousness of God.

Paul begins by showing the universal need for God's righteousness (1-3:20). He next explains the many accomplishments of God's righteousness in Christ (3:21-5:21). He then turns to how we can experience God's righteousness in our own lives (6-8) in a way that transforms the way we look at ourselves, our struggles and our futures. Chapter 8 is the summit of this transformed way of looking at our lives: none of our past sins, present struggles or future hardships can separate us from the overcoming, always-gracious love of God that has been "poured out" into us through the Holy Spirit.

As you reflect, notice the many experiences that could get the better of us: guilt over past sin; defeat by besetting sins; loneliness and uncertainty; fears about how we might be treated or how we might respond when we are persecuted. Paul finishes by stating, "in all these things we are more than conquerors through him who loved us!" As the Gospel makes its way ever deeper into our thinking, we can look at our own sins, inadequacies and fears and know that God is greater than all of them. *He* will sustain and protect us.

CORRELATION

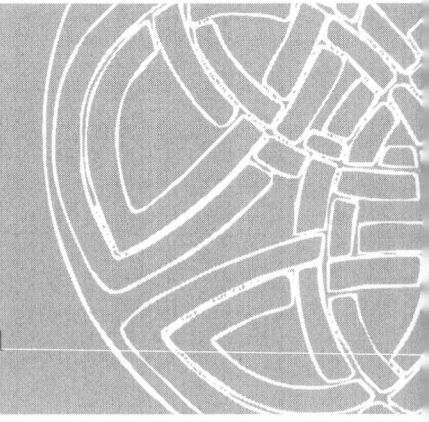

...it is God who makes both us and you stand firm in Christ.

2 Corinthians 1:21

RECITATION

Lord, you have been our dwelling place throughout all generations.

Before the mountains were born or you brought forth the universe, from everlasting to everlasting, you are God.

Forgive us our sins that we might not be consumed by your anger.

Teach us to number our days that we may gain a heart of wisdom.

Satisfy us in the morning with your unfailing love, that we may sing for joy and be glad in all our days.

Heal us and restore us from our afflictions, Lord, for this world is filled with many troubles.

May your favor rest upon us, and may the work of our hands be established by You, Father.

A prayer based on Psalm 90

APPLICATION

What has come to mind, either through the passage or in your reflection that you want to remember?

Fruit of the Spirit

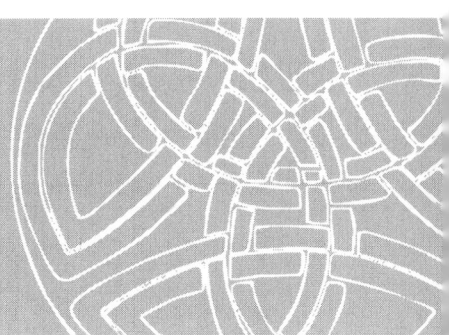

Passage: Galatians 5:13-6:10

Meditation: Galatians 5:13-6:10
Pause and Reflect Silently
Highlight Key Phrases
Look to and Lift up Christ

[13] You, my brothers and sisters, were called to be free. But do not use your freedom to indulge the flesh; rather, serve one another humbly in love. [14] For the entire law is fulfilled in keeping this one command: "Love your neighbor as yourself." [15] If you bite and devour each other, watch out or you will be destroyed by each other.

[16] So I say, walk by the Spirit, and you will not gratify the desires of the flesh. [17] For the flesh desires what is contrary to the Spirit, and the Spirit what is contrary to the flesh. They are in conflict with each other, so that you are not to do whatever you want. [18] But if you are led by the Spirit, you are not under the law. [19] The acts of the flesh are obvious: sexual immorality, impurity and debauchery; [20] idolatry and witchcraft; hatred, discord, jealousy, fits of rage, selfish ambition, dissensions, factions [21] and envy; drunkenness, orgies, and the like. I warn you, as I did before, that those who live like this will not inherit the kingdom of God.

²²*But the fruit of the Spirit is love, joy, peace, forbearance, kindness, goodness, faithfulness,* ²³*gentleness and self-control. Against such things there is no law.* ²⁴*Those who belong to Christ Jesus have crucified the flesh with its passions and desires.* ²⁵*Since we live by the Spirit, let us keep in step with the Spirit.* ²⁶*Let us not become conceited, provoking and envying each other.*

6¹*Brothers and sisters, if someone is caught in a sin, you who live by the Spirit should restore that person gently. But watch yourselves, or you also may be tempted.* ²*Carry each other's burdens, and in this way you will fulfill the law of Christ.*

³*If anyone thinks they are something when they are not, they deceive themselves.* ⁴*Each one should test their own actions. Then they can take pride in themselves alone, without comparing themselves to someone else,* ⁵*for each one should carry their own load.* ⁶*Nevertheless, the one who receives instruction in the word should share all good things with their instructor.*

⁷*Do not be deceived: God cannot be mocked. A man reaps what he sows.* ⁸*Whoever sows to please their flesh, from the flesh will reap destruction; whoever sows to please the Spirit, from the Spirit will reap eternal life.* ⁹*Let us not become weary in doing good, for at the proper time we will reap a harvest if we do not give up.* ¹⁰*Therefore, as we have opportunity, let us do good to all people, especially to those who belong to the family of believers.*

REFLECTION

There are two equally bad paths Christians can take: 1) the path of Legalism and 2) the path of License. Legalism makes the Christian life about law-keeping and elevates it above loving others. It creates a critical, condemning atmosphere in which people "bite and devour each other (5:15)." License makes the Christian life about freedom from restraint and leads to personal immaturity and immorality (5:13, 19-21). Both are unable to overcome the power of sin and help Christians grow into the fullness of the Fruit of the Spirit.

To those who have made grace an excuse for immorality, Paul, in essence, says, "you cannot live like hell and expect to go to heaven!" To those who think that law-keeping (then the Jewish social, dietary and ritual laws of Moses) can make people into godly, mature, other-centered Christ-followers, Paul says, "Wake up! No law has ever made a person a true lover of others."

Paul offers a third path to life: walk in the Spirit. The phrase is a bit vague to our minds today, but we can begin to understand what Paul means when we see that the Spirit brings the Light and Love of God displayed in Christ into our lives (see the passages below). The Spirit provides the insight on how things really are before God and the power we need to become everything God seeks for us to be. It is in trusting these truths and promises that we grow into maturity.

Paul helps define Christian maturity by highlighting nine supernatural qualities. It is important to see that these qualities are *fruit*: They are not directly producible but the indirect result of a healthy tree producing what it was created for! Notice also that he does not say fruits (plural) but *fruit* of the Spirit. We are not embodying the maturity God seeks in our life when we are marked by some of these qualities but only to the extent that we are marked by all of these qualities.

CORRELATION

... God's love has been poured out into our hearts through the Holy Spirit, who has been given to us.
Romans 5:5b

As it is written: "What no eye has seen, what no ear has heard, and what no human mind has conceived"—the things God has prepared for those who love him— these are the things God has revealed to us by his Spirit.
1 Corinthians 2:9-10

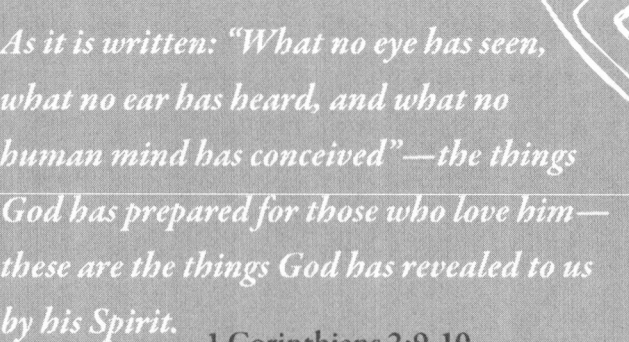

RECITATION

Our Father in Heaven

Hallowed be Your Name

Your Kingdom come,

Your will be done,
 on earth as it is in Heaven.

Give us today our daily bread

Forgive us our debts,
 as we also have forgiven our debtors.

And lead us not into temptation,
 but deliver us from the evil one.

Matthew 6:9-13

APPLICATION

What has come to mind, either through the passage or in your reflection that you want to remember?

The Armor of God

Passage: Ephesians 6:10-20

Meditation: Ephesians 6:10-20
Pause and Reflect Silently
Highlight Key Phrases
Look to and Lift up Christ

[10] Finally, be strong in the Lord and in his mighty power.

[11] Put on the full armor of God, so that you can take your stand against the devil's schemes.

[12] For our struggle is not against flesh and blood,

but against the rulers, against the authorities, against the powers of this dark world and against the spiritual forces of evil in the heavenly realms.

[13] Therefore put on the full armor of God, so that when the day of evil comes, you may be able to stand your ground, and after you have done everything, to stand.

[14] Stand firm then, with the belt of truth buckled around your waist, with the breastplate of righteousness in place, [15] and with your feet fitted with the readiness that comes from the gospel of peace.

[16] In addition to all this, take up the shield of faith, with which you can extinguish all the flaming arrows of the evil one.

[17] Take the helmet of salvation and the sword of the Spirit, which is the word of God.

[18] And pray in the Spirit on all occasions with all kinds of prayers and requests. With this in mind, be alert and always keep on praying for all the Lord's people.

[19] Pray also for me, that whenever I speak, words may be given me so that I will fearlessly make known the mystery of the gospel, [20] for which I am an ambassador in chains. Pray that I may declare it fearlessly, as I should.

REFLECTION

We were born into a battle zone! Like it or not, we are in the middle of a war with life-and-death consequences.

Our world is filled with relational, social, political and military confrontations; Paul wants us to see that these are manifestations of a bigger war taking place "in the heavenly realms."

In our last devotional we read about the sin nature that is in conflict with the Spirit. This is the human dimension of this bigger war. In this passage, Paul focuses on the angelic dimension of this conflict taking place between God and the demonic powers. They are in a mutinous war against God.

Jesus said that the devil, like a thief, had come "only to steal and kill and destroy (John 10:10a)." His darkness and damage had at one point extended into Heaven itself. Yet, a key part of the Good News is that God kicked Satan out of heaven (Rev 12:3-9) and has now taken back the "high ground" in the war. God is on the offensive (Mt 16:18) and is now infiltrating enemy territory through Jesus Christ and his Spirit. Dallas Willard called it a Divine Conspiracy and we have been called to join it! To do so we need to put on "the armor of God."

Using the gear of a typical Roman soldier as a guide, Paul describes the essentials we need to fight victoriously in this fallen world behind enemy lines: the belt of *truth*; the breastplate of *righteousness;* the shoes of *Gospel peace;* the shield of *faith;* the Helmet of *Salvation;* the sword of the Spirit; the *Word of God*. These equip us to fight with God in the world as it truly is. Paul puts special emphasis on standing in this passage. We are not going to win every visible battle, but we can win in the unseen, spiritual war, when we stand firm and true, loyal to Christ through whatever we may face. Paul finishes the passage by focusing on prayer. We need to stay in constant contact with our Commander to sustain our ability to live our lives on the front line.

CORRELATION

After consulting the people, Jehoshaphat appointed men to sing to the Lord and to praise him for the splendor of his holiness as they went out at the head of the army, saying: "Give thanks to the Lord, for his love endures forever."

2 Chronicles 20:21

Hear, Israel: Today you are going into battle against your enemies. Do not be fainthearted or afraid; do not panic or be terrified by them. For the Lord your God is the one who goes with you to fight for you against your enemies to give you victory."

Deuteronomy 2:3-4

RECITATION

Lord Jesus Christ, Son of God, have mercy on me, a sinner.

The Jesus Prayer

> Recite three times slowly.

APPLICATION

What has come to mind, either through the passage or in your reflection that you want to remember?

Rejoice In The Lord

Passage: Philippians 4:4-20

Meditation: Philippians 4:4-20
Pause and Reflect Silently
Highlight Key Phrases
Look to and Lift up Christ

⁴Rejoice in the Lord always. I will say it again: Rejoice! ⁵Let your gentleness be evident to all. The Lord is near.

⁶Do not be anxious about anything, but in every situation, by prayer and petition, with thanksgiving, present your requests to God. ⁷And the peace of God, which transcends all understanding, will guard your hearts and your minds in Christ Jesus.

⁸Finally, brothers and sisters, whatever is true, whatever is noble, whatever is right, whatever is pure, whatever is lovely, whatever is admirable—if anything is excellent or praiseworthy—think about such things. ⁹Whatever you have learned or received or heard from me, or seen in me—put it into practice. And the God of peace will be with you.

¹⁰I rejoiced greatly in the Lord that at last you renewed your concern for me. Indeed, you were concerned, but you had no opportunity to show it. ¹¹I am not saying this because I am in need, for I have learned to be content whatever the circumstances.

^{12}*I know what it is to be in need, and I know what it is to have plenty. I have learned the secret of being content in any and every situation, whether well fed or hungry, whether living in plenty or in want.* ^{13}*I can do all this through him who gives me strength.*

^{14}*Yet it was good of you to share in my troubles.* ^{15}*Moreover, as you Philippians know, in the early days of your acquaintance with the gospel, when I set out from Macedonia, not one church shared with me in the matter of giving and receiving, except you only;* ^{16}*for even when I was in Thessalonica, you sent me aid more than once when I was in need.*

^{17}*Not that I desire your gifts; what I desire is that more be credited to your account.* ^{18}*I have received full payment and have more than enough. I am amply supplied, now that I have received from Epaphroditus the gifts you sent. They are a fragrant offering, an acceptable sacrifice, pleasing to God.* ^{19}*And my God will meet all your needs according to the riches of his glory in Christ Jesus.*

^{20}*To our God and Father be glory forever and ever. Amen.*

REFLECTION

"Rejoice in the Lord always; I will say it again: Rejoice! Whatever you have learned or received or heard from me, or seen in me—*put it into practice.*" Christianity is more than a belief system, more than a moral code; more than a spiritual battle: it is a relationship with the living, loving, infinite God of creation who wants to spend eternity with us! So many things distract us from this wonderful truth.

Paul lived in the fullness of God and could honestly say that knowing Christ was the driving desire of his life (Ph 3:7-8). He wanted the Philippians to live in that same fullness and shared his "secrets" with them. To do so they needed to accept that knowing God did not come effortlessly. To live in the wonder and warmth of knowing Christ, they, and we, need to *work at it*. We naturally drift away from God and get caught up in lesser things that weaken and degrade us.

Being a Christian is like being given a free membership in the best gym in town. It has been gifted to us but we have to go there, time and again, to enjoy the benefit. And when we go we need to work out even when we don't feel like it. Going to the gym and spending an hour gazing off into space will not change us. But if we go *and* work out we will soon see the differences in our life, mentally, emotionally, spiritually and even relationally.

So how do we work out? Paul focuses on celebrating God, appreciating His beauty in the creation, strengthening your patience, praying about everything, meditating on good and godly things, and caring for other Christians in need. Do these things *over and over again* and the God of peace will be with you! You will know God in a way that transforms your character and brings contentment. There are no shortcuts to getting and staying fit, and there are no substitutes for these practices that pull us out of our laziness and sinfulness to help us develop a disciplined life centered on and rooted in God.

CORRELATION

Therefore, my dear friends, as you have always obeyed— not only in my presence, but now much more in my absence—continue to work out your salvation with fear and trembling, for it is God who works in you to will and to act in order to fulfill his good purpose.

Philippians 2:12-13

RECITATION

I believe in God the Father, Almighty Maker of heaven and earth.

And in Jesus Christ his only Son our Lord; who was conceived by the Holy Spirit,

born of the Virgin Mary, suffered under Pontius Pilate, was crucified, dead, and buried; he descended into hell; the third day he rose again from the dead;

He ascended into heaven, and sits on the right hand of God the Father Almighty; from there he shall come to judge the living and the dead.

I believe in the Holy Spirit; the holy Christian Church; the communion of saints; the forgiveness of sins; the resurrection of the body; and the life everlasting. AMEN.

The Apostle's Creed

APPLICATION

What has come to mind, either through the passage or in your reflection that you want to remember?

The Supremacy of Christ

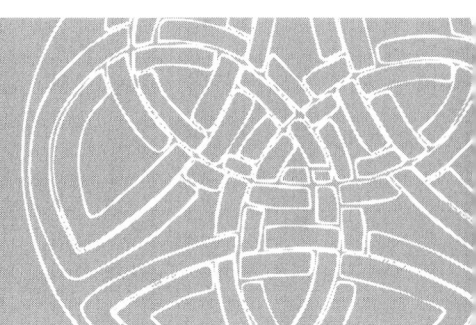

Passage: Colossians 1:1-23

Meditation: Colossians 1:3-23
Pause and Reflect Silently
Highlight Key Phrases
Look to and Lift up Christ

³*We always thank God, the Father of our Lord Jesus Christ, when we pray for you, ⁴because we have heard of your faith in Christ Jesus and of the love you have for all God's people—⁵the faith and love that spring from the hope stored up for you in heaven and about which you have already heard in the true message of the gospel ⁶that has come to you.*

In the same way, the gospel is bearing fruit and growing throughout the whole world—just as it has been doing among you since the day you heard it and truly understood God's grace. ⁷You learned it from Epaphras, our dear fellow servant, who is a faithful minister of Christ on our behalf, ⁸and who also told us of your love in the Spirit.

⁹*For this reason, since the day we heard about you, we have not stopped praying for you. We continually ask God to fill you with the knowledge of his will through all the wisdom and understanding that the Spirit gives,*

¹⁰so that you may live a life worthy of the Lord and please him in every way: bearing fruit in every good work, growing in the knowledge of God, ¹¹being strengthened with all power according to his glorious might so that you may have great endurance and patience, ¹²and giving joyful thanks to the Father, who has qualified you to share in the inheritance of his holy people in the kingdom of light. ¹³For he has rescued us from the dominion of darkness and brought us into the kingdom of the Son he loves, ¹⁴in whom we have redemption, the forgiveness of sins.

¹⁵The Son is the image of the invisible God, the firstborn over all creation. ¹⁶For in him all things were created: things in heaven and on earth, visible and invisible, whether thrones or powers or rulers or authorities; all things have been created through him and for him. ¹⁷He is before all things, and in him all things hold together. ¹⁸And he is the head of the body, the church; he is the beginning and the firstborn from among the dead, so that in everything he might have the supremacy.

¹⁹For God was pleased to have all his fullness dwell in him, ²⁰and through him to reconcile to himself all things, whether things on earth or things in heaven, by making peace through his blood, shed on the cross. ²¹Once you were alienated from God and were enemies in your minds because of your evil behavior. ²²But now he has reconciled you by Christ's physical body through death to present you holy in his sight, without blemish and free from accusation—²³if you continue in your faith, established and firm, and do not move from the hope held out in the gospel. This is the gospel that you heard and that has

been proclaimed to every creature under heaven, and of which I, Paul, have become a servant.

REFLECTION

"Jesus is not one in the group of the world's great. Talk about Alexander the Great and Charles the Great and Napoleon the Great if you will...Jesus is apart. He is not the Great – He is the only."[19] This quote from Carnegie Simpson reminds us that Jesus Christ is in a category all his own.

Jesus was fully human but not merely human. He was a Divine person who took on human nature. Because of this we cannot fall into the habit of thinking of Jesus Christ as one religious leader among many. He is God come to earth to reclaim His own. C.S. Lewis put it well when he said, "'I'm ready to accept Jesus as a great moral teacher, but I don't accept His claim to be God.' That is the one thing we must not say. A man who was merely a man and said the sort of things Jesus said would not be a great moral teacher. He would either be a lunatic--on a level with the man who says he is a poached egg--or else he would be the Devil of Hell. You must make your choice. Either this man was, and is, the Son of God; or else a madman or something worse. You can shut Him up for a fool, you can spit at Him and kill Him as a demon, or you can fall at His feet and call Him Lord and God. But let us not come with any patronizing nonsense about His being a great moral human teacher. He has not left that open to us. He did not intend to."[20]

Our passage is one of the most meaty and insightful found in the New Testament. Every phrase deserves a sermon. Running through it is the golden thread of the Gospel: the good news of what God has done and achieved through the life and work of Jesus Christ.

Paul specially emphasizes the hope of the Gospel in this passage. When we falter in our faith in Christ or when our love for other Christians goes dry we need to regain our vision of the glorious hope we have in Christ, the Savior of mankind, the Divine Son, the Image of God, and the Head of the Church.

CORRELATION

Jesus answered: "Don't you know me, Philip, even after I have been among you such a long time? Anyone who has seen me has seen the Father. How can you say, 'Show us the Father'?

John 14:9

RECITATION

O Father, light up
   the small duties of this day's life;

May they shine
   with the beauty of Your countenance.

May we believe that glory can dwell
   in the commonest task of every day.

Augustine of Hippo

APPLICATION

What has come to mind, either through the passage or in your reflection that you want to remember?

Elders and Deacons

Passage: 1 Timothy 3:1-16

Meditation: 1 Timothy 3:1-16
Pause and Reflect Silently
Highlight Key Phrases
Look to and Lift up Christ

¹*Here is a trustworthy saying: Whoever aspires to be an overseer desires a noble task.*

²*Now the overseer is to be above reproach, faithful to his wife, temperate, self-controlled, respectable, hospitable, able to teach,* ³*not given to drunkenness, not violent but gentle, not quarrelsome, not a lover of money.*

⁴*He must manage his own family well and see that his children obey him, and he must do so in a manner worthy of full respect.* ⁵*(If anyone does not know how to manage his own family, how can he take care of God's church?)*

⁶*He must not be a recent convert, or he may become conceited and fall under the same judgment as the devil.* ⁷*He must also have a good reputation with outsiders, so that he will not fall into disgrace and into the devil's trap.*

⁸*In the same way, deacons are to be worthy of respect, sincere,*

not indulging in much wine, and not pursuing dishonest gain. ⁹They must keep hold of the deep truths of the faith with a clear conscience. ¹⁰They must first be tested; and then if there is nothing against them, let them serve as deacons.

¹¹In the same way, the women are to be worthy of respect, not malicious talkers but temperate and trustworthy in everything.

¹²A deacon must be faithful to his wife and must manage his children and his household well. ¹³Those who have served well gain an excellent standing and great assurance in their faith in Christ Jesus.

¹⁴Although I hope to come to you soon, I am writing you these instructions so that, ¹⁵if I am delayed, you will know how people ought to conduct themselves in God's household, which is the church of the living God, the pillar and foundation of the truth. ¹⁶Beyond all question, the mystery from which true godliness springs is great:

> He appeared in the flesh,
>   was vindicated by the Spirit,
> was seen by angels,
>   was preached among the nations,
> was believed on in the world,
>   was taken up in glory.

REFLECTION

As we read through the book of Acts we saw different types of leaders introduced: Apostles (Peter and John), Deacons (Stephen), Evangelists (Philip), Prophets (Agabus), Teachers (Barnabas and Apollos), and Elders (like those in Jerusalem and Ephesus). These roles were not hard and fast. Philip was also one of the first Deacons and Paul functioned as an Apostle, evangelist, prophet, and teacher.

1 Timothy is one of the last New Testament letters written. By the time Paul wrote Timothy this letter, the church had grown from being a pioneer movement led by Apostles and prophets into a more established movement that needed local leaders acting as elders and deacons. As that first generation of leaders began passing away it was essential that a new generation of leaders be prepared and commissioned for ministry. Paul gives Timothy the instruction he needs to appoint elders and deacons in Ephesus (1:3). Elders were also called overseers, shepherds and pastors. Deacons took care of the practical and monetary needs of the people.

In our passage we see Paul raising a high bar for those in leadership. Why? An organization's future depends on the quality and maturity of its leaders. We are called to do everything in a way that points beyond ourselves to God (1 Co 10:31) and followers will rarely exceed their leaders. If the leaders have not yet learned to glorify God through their lifestyle it is very unlikely that their followers will either! As Paul checks off the essential qualities of Christian leadership he focuses on issues related to proven character, relational wisdom and theological conviction. One key word that might summarize the list is *loyalty*: a Christian leader must have a proven track record of being loyal to our Savior, his spouse and the Scriptures.

CORRELATION

So Christ himself gave the apostles, the prophets, the evangelists, the pastors and teachers, to equip his people for works of service, so that the body of Christ may be built up until we all reach unity in the faith and in the knowledge of the Son of God and become mature, attaining to the whole measure of the fullness of Christ. Ephesians 4:11-13

RECITATION

LORD, MAKE ME AN INSTRUMENT OF YOUR PEACE,

where there is hatred, let me sow love,

where there is injury, pardon,

where there is discord, may I bring harmony,

where there is error, may I bring truth,

where there is doubt, may I bring faith,

where there is despair, may I bring hope,

where there is darkness, may I bring light,

and where there is sadness, may I bring joy.

O Divine Master,

grant that I may not so much seek

To be consoled, as to console,

to be understood, as to understand,

to be loved, as to love.

for it is in giving that we receive;

it is in pardoning that we are pardoned;

and it is in dying that we are born into eternal life.

Francis of Assisi

APPLICATION

What has come to mind, either through the passage or in your reflection that you want to remember?

The Love of Money

Passage: 1 Timothy 6:3-21

Meditation: 1 Timothy 6:3-21
Pause and Reflect Silently
Highlight Key Phrases
Look to and Lift up Christ

³If anyone teaches otherwise and does not agree to the sound instruction of our Lord Jesus Christ and to godly teaching, ⁴they are conceited and understand nothing. They have an unhealthy interest in controversies and quarrels about words that result in envy, strife, malicious talk, evil suspicions ⁵and constant friction between people of corrupt mind, who have been robbed of the truth and who think that godliness is a means to financial gain.

⁶But godliness with contentment is great gain. ⁷For we brought nothing into the world, and we can take nothing out of it. ⁸But if we have food and clothing, we will be content with that.

⁹Those who want to get rich fall into temptation and a trap and into many foolish and harmful desires that plunge people into ruin and destruction. ¹⁰For the love of money is a root of all kinds of evil. Some people, eager for money, have wandered from the faith and pierced themselves with many griefs.

¹¹But you, man of God, flee from all this, and pursue righteous-

ness, godliness, faith, love, endurance and gentleness. [12]Fight the good fight of the faith. Take hold of the eternal life to which you were called when you made your good confession in the presence of many witnesses.

[13]In the sight of God, who gives life to everything, and of Christ Jesus, who while testifying before Pontius Pilate made the good confession, I charge you [14]to keep this command without spot or blame until the appearing of our Lord Jesus Christ, [15]which God will bring about in his own time—God, the blessed and only Ruler, the King of kings and Lord of lords, [16]who alone is immortal and who lives in unapproachable light, whom no one has seen or can see. To him be honor and might forever. Amen.

[17]Command those who are rich in this present world not to be arrogant nor to put their hope in wealth, which is so uncertain, but to put their hope in God, who richly provides us with everything for our enjoyment. [18]Command them to do good, to be rich in good deeds, and to be generous and willing to share. [19]In this way they will lay up treasure for themselves as a firm foundation for the coming age, so that they may take hold of the life that is truly life.

[20]Timothy, guard what has been entrusted to your care. Turn away from godless chatter and the opposing ideas of what is falsely called knowledge, [21]which some have professed and in so doing have departed from the faith.

Grace be with you all.

REFLECTION

We live in a world filled with uncertainties, dangers and injustices, as well as pleasures, technological advances and beauty. Where do we turn to find our sense of security in such a world? Where do we seek our satisfaction? And how do we define our success?

The natural human tendency is to seek these things in money and what it can bring to our life. Giving in to this temptation has dire consequences. Paul says that greed can "plunge people into ruin" and rob them of the truth, so that they pierce "themselves with many griefs." Do you see the irony? Seeking your security, satisfaction and success in money actually leads to the very things you hope to avoid!

Greed, when wedded to our Christian faith, makes us vulnerable to the temptation of using the Christian community as a means to personal wealth. The fact that there were Christian leaders in Ephesus taking advantage of people's greed made the situation even more difficult. Paul commands Timothy to do what is necessary to excise this moral cancer from the church. The price of not doing so would have both earthly and eternal consequences.

Does this mean that money is evil in itself? No! It is the *love of money* that is the root of all kinds of evil. The material world is not evil but when we seek our life in it our desires take on a power of their own. God is meant to be the source of our security and satisfaction, and He alone defines true success for us.

The allure of money though, is overwhelming, and we cannot overcome it overnight. But if we want to hear our heavenly Father say, "Well done" we must do so. Where do we start? By seeing that our heart follows where our money goes. Learn to give freely, then proportionally (a 10% tithe is a great place to start), then generously and sacrificially and you will break the bonds money has over you and discover just how wonderful "godliness with contentment" can be as a way of life.

CORRELATION

No one can serve two masters. Either you will hate the one and love the other, or you will be devoted to the one and despise the other. You cannot serve both God and money. Matthew 6:24

One man gives freely, yet gains even more: another withholds unduly, but comes to poverty. A generous man will prosper; he who refreshes others will himself be refreshed. Proverbs 11:24-25

RECITATION

Thanks be to you, our Lord Jesus Christ,

For all the benefits you have given us,

For all the pains and insults you have borne for us.

Most merciful Redeemer, Friend, and Brother,

May we know you more clearly,

Love you more dearly,

And follow you more nearly:

Forever and ever. AMEN.

Richard Chichester

APPLICATION

What has come to mind, either through the passage or in your reflection that you want to remember?

Good Soldiers of Christ

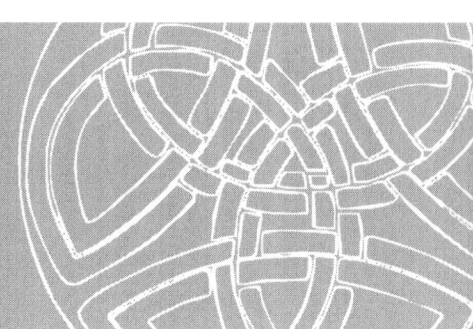

Passage: 2 Timothy 2:1-26

Meditation: 2 Timothy 2:1-21
Pause and Reflect Silently
Highlight Key Phrases
Look to and Lift up Christ

¹*You then, my son, be strong in the grace that is in Christ Jesus.* ²*And the things you have heard me say in the presence of many witnesses entrust to reliable people who will also be qualified to teach others.* ³*Join with me in suffering, like a good soldier of Christ Jesus.* ⁴*No one serving as a soldier gets entangled in civilian affairs, but rather tries to please his commanding officer.* ⁵*Similarly, anyone who competes as an athlete does not receive the victor's crown except by competing according to the rules.* 6 *The hardworking farmer should be the first to receive a share of the crops.* ⁷*Reflect on what I am saying, for the Lord will give you insight into all this.*

⁸*Remember Jesus Christ, raised from the dead, descended from David. This is my gospel,* ⁹*for which I am suffering even to the point of being chained like a criminal. But God's word is not chained.* ¹⁰*Therefore I endure everything for the sake of the elect, that they too may obtain the salvation that is in Christ Jesus, with eternal glory.*

¹¹Here is a trustworthy saying:

> If we died with him,
>   we will also live with him;
> ¹²if we endure,
>   we will also reign with him.
> If we disown him,
>   he will also disown us;
> ¹³if we are faithless,
>   he remains faithful,
>   for he cannot disown himself.

¹⁴Keep reminding God's people of these things. Warn them before God against quarreling about words; it is of no value, and only ruins those who listen. ¹⁵Do your best to present yourself to God as one approved, a worker who does not need to be ashamed and who correctly handles the word of truth. ¹⁶Avoid godless chatter, because those who indulge in it will become more and more ungodly. ¹⁷Their teaching will spread like gangrene. Among them are Hymenaeus and Philetus, ¹⁸who have departed from the truth. They say that the resurrection has already taken place, and they destroy the faith of some. ¹⁹Nevertheless, God's solid foundation stands firm, sealed with this inscription: "The Lord knows those who are his," and, "Everyone who confesses the name of the Lord must turn away from wickedness."

²⁰In a large house there are articles not only of gold and silver, but also of wood and clay; some are for special purposes and some for common use. ²¹Those who cleanse themselves from the

latter will be instruments for special purposes, made holy, useful to the Master and prepared to do any good work.

REFLECTION

"Join with me in suffering, like a good soldier of Christ Jesus." This second letter to Timothy was written as Paul was preparing to die for his faith. What would you say to someone you considered to be a son when you knew you had very little time left?

Paul gives Timothy the advice he will need to persevere in the darkening days that lay ahead. He challenges Timothy to keep advancing in his pastoral ministry in spite of what was happening to himself. He gives Timothy six pieces of advice in this chapter, and their order may be as important as their content. *First*, remember to care for your own soul. *Second*, remember the Good News about Jesus Christ. *Third*, don't get caught up in worthless controversies. *Fourth*, live a noble life that pleases your Master. *Fifth*, flee the evil desires of youth. *Sixth*, treat people with kindness and respect, especially when you are in a position of authority.

Interestingly, Paul starts by telling Timothy to keep in touch with his own personal growth ("grow strong in grace") and personal devotion to Christ (like a soldier, like an athlete, like a farmer). Our circumstances can drain and dishearten us if we are not careful to stay rooted and grounded in Christ.

Paul ends by giving Timothy timeless advice that every leader needs to remember, regardless of the size of their ministry. He describes how servant leaders should respond when people criticize or seek to undermine their teaching. Not with harshness or condemnation. Not with defensiveness or accusations. They are to keep sharing God's truth with gentleness and consistency and remind themselves that the person in front of them has very possibly been deceived by the adversary, the devil. These are the practices that help leaders persevere when times get tough and they and their friends are going through painful circumstances.

CORRELATION

Watch your life and doctrine closely. Persevere in them, because if you do, you will save both yourself and your hearers.
1 Timothy 4:16

RECITATION

Lord, whatever this day may bring

Your name be praised.

Be gracious to me and help me.

Grant me strength to bear whatever you may send,

And let not fear overrule me.

I trust your grace and commit my life wholly into your hands.

Whether I live or whether I die, I am with you.

And you are with me,

O my Lord and my God.

Lord, I wait for your salvation,
   and for the coming of your kingdom. Amen

Dietrich Bonhoeffer

APPLICATION

What has come to mind, either through the passage or in your reflection that you want to remember?

Scripture is God-Breathed

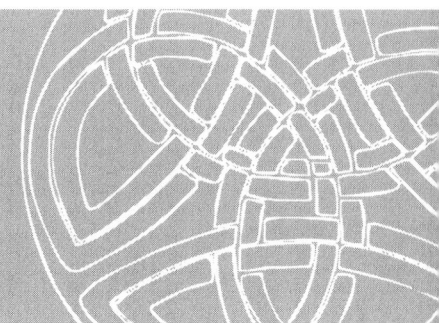

Passage: 2 Timothy 3:10-4:8

Meditation: 2 Timothy 3:10-4:8
Pause and Reflect Silently
Highlight Key Phrases
Look to and Lift up Christ

¹⁰You, however, know all about my teaching, my way of life, my purpose, faith, patience, love, endurance, ¹¹persecutions, sufferings—what kinds of things happened to me in Antioch, Iconium and Lystra, the persecutions I endured.

Yet the Lord rescued me from all of them. ¹²In fact, everyone who wants to live a godly life in Christ Jesus will be persecuted, ¹³while evildoers and impostors will go from bad to worse, deceiving and being deceived.

¹⁴But as for you, continue in what you have learned and have become convinced of, because you know those from whom you learned it, ¹⁵and how from infancy you have known the Holy Scriptures, which are able to make you wise for salvation through faith in Christ Jesus.

¹⁶All Scripture is God-breathed and is useful for teaching, rebuking, correcting and training in righteousness, ¹⁷so that the servant of God may be thoroughly equipped for every good work.

4 ¹*In the presence of God and of Christ Jesus, who will judge the living and the dead, and in view of his appearing and his kingdom, I give you this charge: ²Preach the word; be prepared in season and out of season; correct, rebuke and encourage—with great patience and careful instruction.*

³*For the time will come when people will not put up with sound doctrine. Instead, to suit their own desires, they will gather around them a great number of teachers to say what their itching ears want to hear. ⁴They will turn their ears away from the truth and turn aside to myths.*

⁵*But you, keep your head in all situations, endure hardship, do the work of an evangelist, discharge all the duties of your ministry.*

⁶*For I am already being poured out like a drink offering, and the time for my departure is near. ⁷I have fought the good fight, I have finished the race, I have kept the faith.*

⁸*Now there is in store for me the crown of righteousness, which the Lord, the righteous Judge, will award to me on that day—and not only to me, but also to all who have longed for his appearing.*

REFLECTION

Timothy grew up in a city that Paul visited on his first missionary journey (Lystra) and joined him in his travels on his second missionary journey (Acts 16:1). During Paul's third missionary journey, Timothy was repeatedly sent out as a leader to take care of hot-spots that needed more direct oversight (e.g. 1 Corinthians 4:17). Thus Timothy had first-hand knowledge, experience and training that had developed under nearly 20 years of Paul's ministry leadership. He wasn't naive about the challenges and he knew the price many had already paid for their faith.

Paul, though, did not want Timothy to center his life on him but on God and His inspired Word. *Scripture* in this passage refers to what we call the Old Testament. The books of the New Testament were written and overseen by the original Apostles and have always been accepted as fully inspired as well.

The term *God-breathed* gets to the truth that all of Scripture flows outward from God (think how you breathe out whenever you speak) and is not the self-generated thoughts of human beings. Paul wants Timothy to see that it is God's Word that ultimately teaches us, convicts us, corrects us and trains us. We need to accept the divine authority and supernatural ability of Scripture to truly and enduringly know, serve and glorify God.

The deeper our confidence in Scripture's power, the more we will be able to courageously face life and its many challenges (3:14). As Paul wrote to Timothy he was in a jail: isolated, trapped, and feeling very alone. But he gained great assurance in knowing the spiritual heritage that Timothy had through his mother and grandmother (3:15). The same is meant to be true of us all: we are to be deeply grateful for the people God has used in our lives, but we are to be even more deeply grateful for His Word which is able to transform and sustain our lives.

CORRELATION

For the word of God is alive and active. Sharper than any double-edged sword, it penetrates even to dividing soul and spirit, joints and marrow; it judges the thoughts and attitudes of the heart. Hebrews 4:12

RECITATION

GOD, GRANT ME THE SERENITY
  to accept the things I cannot change;

Courage to change the things I can and
  the wisdom to know the difference.

To live one day at a time;
  enjoying one moment at a time;

Accepting hardship as the pathway to peace.

To take, as He did, this sinful world as it is, not as I would
  have it.

Trusting that He will make all things right if I surrender to
  His Will.

That I may be reasonably happy in this life and supremely
  happy with You forever in the next. Amen

Reinhold Neibuhr

APPLICATION

What has come to mind, either through the passage or in your reflection that you want to remember?

The Second Coming of Christ

Passage: 1 Thessalonians 4:13-5:11

Meditation: 1 Thessalonians 4:13-5:11
Pause and Reflect Silently
Highlight Key Phrases
Look to and Lift up Christ

¹³*Brothers and sisters, we do not want you to be uninformed about those who sleep in death, so that you do not grieve like the rest of mankind, who have no hope.*

¹⁴*For we believe that Jesus died and rose again, and so we believe that God will bring with Jesus those who have fallen asleep in him.* ¹⁵*According to the Lord's word, we tell you that we who are still alive, who are left until the coming of the Lord, will certainly not precede those who have fallen asleep.*

¹⁶*For the Lord himself will come down from heaven, with a loud command, with the voice of the archangel and with the trumpet call of God, and the dead in Christ will rise first.* ¹⁷*After that, we who are still alive and are left will be caught up together with them in the clouds to meet the Lord in the air. And so we will be with the Lord forever.* ¹⁸*Therefore encourage one another with these words.*

⁵¹Now, brothers and sisters, about times and dates we do not need to write to you, ²for you know very well that the day of the Lord will come like a thief in the night. ³While people are saying, "Peace and safety," destruction will come on them suddenly, as labor pains on a pregnant woman, and they will not escape.

⁴But you, brothers and sisters, are not in darkness so that this day should surprise you like a thief. ⁵You are all children of the light and children of the day. We do not belong to the night or to the darkness.

⁶So then, let us not be like others, who are asleep, but let us be awake and sober. ⁷For those who sleep, sleep at night, and those who get drunk, get drunk at night.

⁸But since we belong to the day, let us be sober, putting on faith and love as a breastplate, and the hope of salvation as a helmet.

⁹For God did not appoint us to suffer wrath but to receive salvation through our Lord Jesus Christ. ¹⁰He died for us so that, whether we are awake or asleep, we may live together with him.

¹¹Therefore encourage one another and build each other up, just as in fact you are doing.

REFLECTION

The first "coming" of Christ began in a manger about 2000 years ago. The second coming of Christ will come just as surely as the first but it will be unmistakable and unavoidable when it happens. There will be no doubt that it is Jesus, the Risen Lord, standing suddenly upon the earth with his glorious angels. His coming will be visible, physical and victorious. Everyone and everything will bow before Him. His coming will not be just a personal realization of his importance, or a "spiritual" awareness of his victory, or a slow transition into a human golden age.

The Bible is clear about the splendor of Christ's second coming. But there is great debate on what will come just before and just after it. If you have been in church for a while you are aware of the terms people use. "Are you pre-trib or post-trib?" "Are you "pre-Mil or a-Mil?" You may remember the End Times craze of the 70's or the "88 reasons why Jesus is coming back in 1988." All of this has led to a new phrase, "I am pan-trib: I believe it will all pan out in the end!"

The details of what will happen just before and just after His return are important and they can challenge us to dive more deeply into Scripture, but we need to keep Christ's Second Coming at the center of our thoughts and hopes.

Mankind, on its own, will never outgrow or develop beyond our innate slavery to sin. It will always cause problems. Fallen human beings will continue to make foolish decisions and at times do truly evil, despicable things. If we place our hope in the ultimate self-perfection of mankind we will repeatedly be disheartened and tend toward despair.

But if we keep our focus on the certainty of Christ's Second Coming we will be able to appreciate the many lives He is changing and know that the best moments we have here are just a foretaste of the joy and glory that awaits us.

CORRELATION

... The Lord Jesus [will be] revealed from heaven in blazing fire with his powerful angels. He will punish those who do not know God and do not obey the gospel of our Lord Jesus... on the day he comes to be glorified in his holy people and to be marveled at among all those who have believed. This includes you, because you believed our testimony to you.

2 Thessalonians 1:7b-10

RECITATION

Father, we give you thanks for all the gifts you freely bestow on us. For the beauty and wonder of your creation, in earth and sky and sea, Lord, we thank you.

For our daily food and drink, our homes and families, and our friends, Lord, we thank you.

For minds to think, and hearts to love, and hands to serve, Lord, we thank you. For health and strength to work, and leisure to rest and play, Lord, we thank you.

For the brave and courageous, who are patient in suffering and faithful in adversity, Lord, we thank you.

For the communion of saints, in all times and places, Lord, we thank you.

Above all, we give you thanks for the great mercies and promises given to us in Christ Jesus our Lord; to him be praise and glory, with you, O Father, and the Holy Spirit, now and forever. AMEN.

APPLICATION

What has come to mind, either through the passage or in your reflection that you want to remember?

The Most Excellent Way

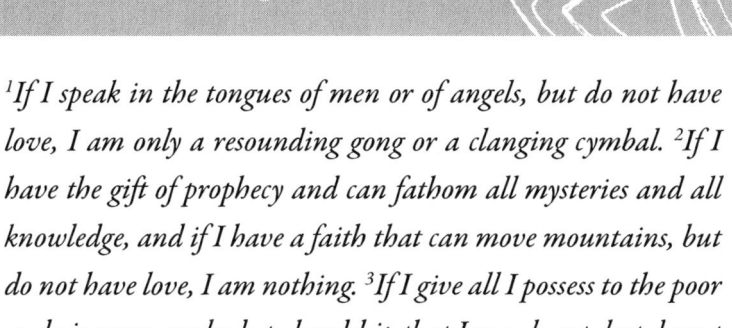

Passage: 1 Corinthians 13:1-13

Meditation: 1 Corinthians 13:1-13
Pause and Reflect Silently
Highlight Key Phrases
Look to and Lift up Christ

¹*If I speak in the tongues of men or of angels, but do not have love, I am only a resounding gong or a clanging cymbal.* ²*If I have the gift of prophecy and can fathom all mysteries and all knowledge, and if I have a faith that can move mountains, but do not have love, I am nothing.* ³*If I give all I possess to the poor and give over my body to hardship that I may boast, but do not have love, I gain nothing.*

⁴*Love is patient, love is kind. It does not envy, it does not boast, it is not proud.* ⁵*It does not dishonor others, it is not self-seeking, it is not easily angered, it keeps no record of wrongs.* ⁶*Love does not delight in evil but rejoices with the truth.* ⁷*It always protects, always trusts, always hopes, always perseveres.*

⁸*Love never fails. But where there are prophecies, they will cease; where there are tongues, they will be stilled; where there is knowledge, it will pass away.* ⁹*For we know in part and we prophesy in part,* ¹⁰*but when completeness comes, what is in part disappears.* ¹¹*When I was a child, I talked like a child, I*

thought like a child, I reasoned like a child. When I became a man, I put the ways of childhood behind me. [12]*For now we see only a reflection as in a mirror; then we shall see face to face. Now I know in part; then I shall know fully, even as I am fully known.*

[13]*And now these three remain: faith, hope and love. But the greatest of these is love.*

REFLECTION

What is the best way to live life? We are *already* being guided by the way we have answered that question. Some live from one experience to another: they believe the best way to live is to get the most out of the moment without thought for the future. Their motto is *carpe diem*, seize the day! But many of them end up being seized, not by joy, but by their own desires, weaknesses and emptiness.

Others want more security: they are anxiously trying to build a wall of protection against life's hardships and losses. Many want personal fame: they want to be known and admired by others. Still others live to accumulate power: they want more control over their own life and the lives of others.

The vast majority of us are a mixture of these. Yet Jesus rejected these motivations in his wilderness temptations (Matt 4) and Paul tells us that they are ultimately pointless. The best way to live life is to learn to be guided by and formed by "agape" love. Paul gives us the qualities that mark the person who has made loving God and others their way of life. Such a person will increasingly exhibit patience, kindness, meekness, forgiveness, justice, trust, and hope.

If we want to become such a person, we need to reject more and more deeply the lures of self-indulgence, self-protection, self-glorification and self-manipulation. We do so to embrace a life of dependence on God and interdependence with other Christians. From the outside this looks a little like death, and in fact, it feels like we are "dying," but the truth is that we are finally entering into life; the eternal kind of life that marks God in His self-giving, other-promoting love within the Trinity.

When we think of heaven we often think of it as a place where every whim and desire of ours is satisfied. The reality is that heaven is the place where everyone loves God and each other like God Himself. Is that the place you are getting yourself ready for?

CORRELATION

Anyone who hates a brother or sister is a murderer, and you know that no murderer has eternal life residing in him. This is how we know what love is: Jesus Christ laid down his life for us. And we ought to lay down our lives for our brothers and sisters. If anyone has material possessions and sees a brother or sister in need but has no pity on them, how can the love of God be in that person?

1 John 3:15-17

RECITATION

Lord, you have been our dwelling place throughout all generations.

Before the mountains were born or you brought forth the universe, from everlasting to everlasting, you are God.

Forgive us our sins that we might not be consumed by your anger.

Teach us to number our days that we may gain a heart of wisdom.

Satisfy us in the morning with your unfailing love, that we may sing for joy and be glad in all our days.

Heal us and restore us from our afflictions, Lord, for this world is filled with many troubles.

May your favor rest upon us, and may the work of our hands be established by you, Father.

A prayer based on Psalm 90

APPLICATION

What has come to mind, either through the passage or in your reflection that you want to remember?

A New Creation in Christ

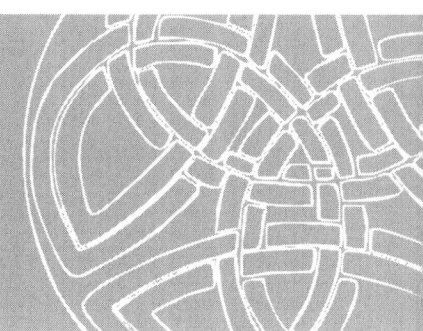

Passage: 2 Corinthians 4:1-6:2

Meditation: 2 Corinthians 5:1-21
Pause and Reflect Silently
Highlight Key Phrases
Look to and Lift up Christ

¹*For we know that if the earthly tent we live in is destroyed, we have a building from God, an eternal house in heaven, not built by human hands.* ²*Meanwhile we groan, longing to be clothed instead with our heavenly dwelling,* ³*because when we are clothed, we will not be found naked.* ⁴*For while we are in this tent, we groan and are burdened, because we do not wish to be unclothed but to be clothed instead with our heavenly dwelling, so that what is mortal may be swallowed up by life.* ⁵*Now the one who has fashioned us for this very purpose is God, who has given us the Spirit as a deposit, guaranteeing what is to come.*

⁶*Therefore we are always confident and know that as long as we are at home in the body we are away from the Lord.* ⁷*For we live by faith, not by sight.* ⁸*We are confident, I say, and would prefer to be away from the body and at home with the Lord.* ⁹*So we make it our goal to please him, whether we are at home in the body or away from it.*

¹⁰For we must all appear before the judgment seat of Christ, so that each of us may receive what is due us for the things done while in the body, whether good or bad.

¹¹Since, then, we know what it is to fear the Lord, we try to persuade others. What we are is plain to God, and I hope it is also plain to your conscience. ¹²We are not trying to commend ourselves to you again, but are giving you an opportunity to take pride in us, so that you can answer those who take pride in what is seen rather than in what is in the heart.

¹³If we are "out of our mind," as some say, it is for God; if we are in our right mind, it is for you. ¹⁴For Christ's love compels us, because we are convinced that one died for all, and therefore all died. ¹⁵And he died for all, that those who live should no longer live for themselves but for him who died for them and was raised again.

¹⁶So from now on we regard no one from a worldly point of view. Though we once regarded Christ in this way, we do so no longer. ¹⁷Therefore, if anyone is in Christ, the new creation has come: The old has gone, the new is here!

¹⁸All this is from God, who reconciled us to himself through Christ and gave us the ministry of reconciliation: ¹⁹that God was reconciling the world to himself in Christ, not counting people's sins against them. And he has committed to us the message of reconciliation. ²⁰We are therefore Christ's ambassadors, as though God were making his appeal through

us. *We implore you on Christ's behalf: Be reconciled to God.*
²¹God made him who had no sin to be sin for us, so that in him we might become the righteousness of God.

REFLECTION

We ask the question, "Who Am I?" to get to the core of our identity: to define our worth and direction in life. We might say, "I am Bob Smith," but that is our name, not who we are. "I am a teacher." "I am a business owner." "I am a student." These are what we do. "I am an American." This is where we live. "I am Hispanic, or Asian, or African-American." These are where we are from.

We define ourselves through our abilities, appearance, achievements, personal past and heritage. Interestingly, God defines us by none of these! When God answers the question, "Who are you?" for those who have received Jesus Christ as Savior and Lord, he says, "You are my child. You are a son or a daughter of the King!" For those who have not yet done so, God says, "You are a sinner; a rebel, a traitor: you need to accept me and bow before me."

Christians need to renew the way they look at themselves. For those who come from painful pasts and label themselves as losers, victims, or sinners who can't help but sin, God says those labels no longer apply to or define us. We have entered into a new reality.

Spend some time enjoying who you really are in God's eyes.

- I am a new creation. *2 Corinthians 5:17*
- I am a citizen of heaven. *Philippians 3:20*
- I am one of God's precious people. *1 Peter 2:9-10*
- I am God's beloved child not an orphan. *1 John 3:2*
- I am a Saint not a sinner. *Romans 1:7, 5:8*
- I am a Victor not a victim. *Romans 8:37*
- I am a Worshiper not a worrier. *1 Peter 2:9; John 21-24*
- I am God's project not a product of my past. *1 Cor 6:9-11*
- I am God's masterpiece-in-the-making. *Ephesians 2:10*
- I am God's salt and light in the world. *Matt 5:13-16*
- I am Christ's ambassador to the world. *2 Cor 5:18-20*

CORRELATION

See what great love the Father has lavished on us, that we should be called children of God! And that is what we are!
1 John 3:1

RECITATION

Our Father in Heaven

Hallowed be Your Name

Your Kingdom come,

Your will be done,
  on earth as it is in Heaven.

Give us today our daily bread

Forgive us our debts,
  as we also have forgiven our debtors.

And lead us not into temptation,
  but deliver us from the evil one.

Matthew 6:9-13

APPLICATION

What has come to mind, either through the passage or in your reflection that you want to remember?

A Living Hope

Passage: 1 Peter 1:1-2:12

Meditation: 1 Peter 1:3-23
Pause and Reflect Silently
Highlight Key Phrases
Look to and Lift up Christ

³*Praise be to the God and Father of our Lord Jesus Christ! In his great mercy he has given us new birth into a living hope through the resurrection of Jesus Christ from the dead, ⁴and into an inheritance that can never perish, spoil or fade. This inheritance is kept in heaven for you, ⁵who through faith are shielded by God's power until the coming of the salvation that is ready to be revealed in the last time.*

⁶*In all this you greatly rejoice, though now for a little while you may have had to suffer grief in all kinds of trials. ⁷These have come so that the proven genuineness of your faith—of greater worth than gold, which perishes even though refined by fire—may result in praise, glory and honor when Jesus Christ is revealed. ⁸Though you have not seen him, you love him; and even though you do not see him now, you believe in him and are filled with an inexpressible and glorious joy, ⁹for you are receiving the end result of your faith, the salvation of your souls.*

¹⁰*Concerning this salvation, the prophets, who spoke of the grace that was to come to you, searched intently and with the greatest care,* ¹¹*trying to find out the time and circumstances to which the Spirit of Christ in them was pointing when he predicted the sufferings of the Messiah and the glories that would follow.* ¹²*It was revealed to them that they were not serving themselves but you, when they spoke of the things that have now been told you by those who have preached the gospel to you by the Holy Spirit sent from heaven. Even angels long to look into these things.*

¹³*Therefore, with minds that are alert and fully sober, set your hope on the grace to be brought to you when Jesus Christ is revealed at his coming.* ¹⁴*As obedient children, do not conform to the evil desires you had when you lived in ignorance.* ¹⁵*But just as he who called you is holy, so be holy in all you do;* ¹⁶*for it is written: "Be holy, because I am holy."*

¹⁷*Since you call on a Father who judges each person's work impartially, live out your time as foreigners here in reverent fear.* ¹⁸*For you know that it was not with perishable things such as silver or gold that you were redeemed from the empty way of life handed down to you from your ancestors,* ¹⁹*but with the precious blood of Christ, a lamb without blemish or defect.* ²⁰*He was chosen before the creation of the world, but was revealed in these last times for your sake.* ²¹*Through him you believe in God, who raised him from the dead and glorified him, and so your faith and hope are in God.*

²²*Now that you have purified yourselves by obeying the truth*

so that you have sincere love for each other, love one another deeply, from the heart. ²³*For you have been born again, not of perishable seed, but of imperishable, through the living and enduring word of God.*

REFLECTION

Take a moment and savor these phrases: living hope; proven faith; inexpressible joy; reverent fear; sincere love. Can you see yourself embodying these qualities? God can!

If we want to move more deeply into these realities we will need to expand our understanding of salvation. The typical Christian thinks of salvation as being equivalent to conversion. "I was saved when I received Jesus Christ." That moment was only the *beginning* of God's salvation. You are in the process of being saved and will one day be entirely saved!

It is the fullness and certainty of that future salvation that Peter wants us to focus on most. The key word is hope. *Hope* refers to what people live for, look to and long for. It is what keeps people going when times get tough.

We think of a hope as a wish, something we want to happen but have no assurance that it will. The New Testament writers used the word to refer to something that was a certainty. You could count on it and know that you would never lose it.

Peter says that we have entered (been born) into this kind of hope through the resurrection of Jesus Christ. We have been given an exciting certainty that we can bank on: one day we *will* enter into the glorious life and world of Jesus. Peter wants us to understand this, appreciate it and see our life experiences through its lens.

Our minds typically focus on the "grief[s] in all kinds of trials" that we experience. Peter wants us to see the "praise, glory and honor" that awaits those who live for Jesus Christ. Rather than letting our imaginations run away with what might happen in this world we need to discipline our imaginations to dwell on what certainly will happen in the next. It is such thinking that keeps us on track; grounded, growing and glorying in Christ Jesus, through the crazy, unpredictable, and grief-filled world we live in.

CORRELATION

For the message of the cross is foolishness to those who are perishing, but to us who are being saved it is the power of God. For it is written: "I will destroy the wisdom of the wise; the intelligence of the intelligent I will frustrate.
1 Corinthians 1:18-19

Why, my soul, are you downcast? Why so disturbed within me? Put your hope in God, for I will yet praise him, my Savior and my God.
Psalm 42:5

The prospect of the righteous is joy, but the hopes of the wicked come to nothing.
Proverbs 10:28

RECITATION

Lord Jesus Christ, Son of God, have mercy on me, a sinner.

The Jesus Prayer

> Recite three times slowly.

APPLICATION

What has come to mind, either through the passage or in your reflection that you want to remember?

Faith and Works

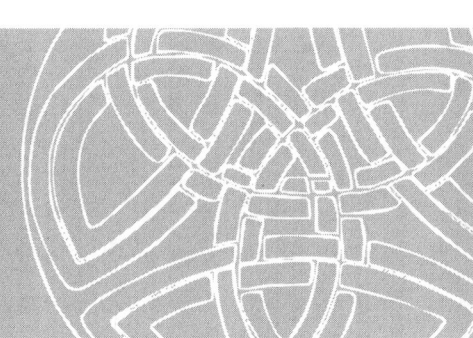

Passage: James 1:1-2:26

Meditation: James 2:8-26
Pause and Reflect Silently
Highlight Key Phrases
Look to and Lift up Christ

⁸If you really keep the royal law found in Scripture, "Love your neighbor as yourself," you are doing right. ⁹But if you show favoritism, you sin and are convicted by the law as lawbreakers.

¹⁰For whoever keeps the whole law and yet stumbles at just one point is guilty of breaking all of it. ¹¹For he who said, "You shall not commit adultery," also said, "You shall not murder." If you do not commit adultery but do commit murder, you have become a lawbreaker.

¹²Speak and act as those who are going to be judged by the law that gives freedom, ¹³because judgment without mercy will be shown to anyone who has not been merciful. Mercy triumphs over judgment.

¹⁴What good is it, my brothers and sisters, if someone claims to have faith but has no deeds? Can such faith save them?

¹⁵Suppose a brother or a sister is without clothes and daily food.

[16]*If one of you says to them, "Go in peace; keep warm and well fed," but does nothing about their physical needs, what good is it?* [17]*In the same way, faith by itself, if it is not accompanied by action, is dead.*

[18]*But someone will say, "You have faith; I have deeds."*

Show me your faith without deeds, and I will show you my faith by my deeds. [19]*You believe that there is one God. Good! Even the demons believe that—and shudder.*

[20]*You foolish person, do you want evidence that faith without deeds is useless?* [21]*Was not our father Abraham considered righteous for what he did when he offered his son Isaac on the altar?* [22]*You see that his faith and his actions were working together, and his faith was made complete by what he did.* [23]*And the scripture was fulfilled that says, "Abraham believed God, and it was credited to him as righteousness," and he was called God's friend.* [24]*You see that a person is considered righteous by what they do and not by faith alone.*

[25]*In the same way, was not even Rahab the prostitute considered righteous for what she did when she gave lodging to the spies and sent them off in a different direction?* [26]*As the body without the spirit is dead, so faith without deeds is dead.*

REFLECTION

In the Sermon on the Mount Jesus said something that should cause each of us to search our souls. He says that not everyone who calls him "Lord" will enter into the eternal kingdom of God (Matt 7:21-23). On that Day people who thought they had done their religious duty or who had done spectacular things in Jesus' name will stand before him and Jesus will say, "I never knew you." That phrase should send a chill down our spines and prod us to make certain that we have truly received Jesus as the Savior and Lord of life.

The New Testament writers challenged people to make sure they had a genuine faith in Jesus Christ. James says bluntly, "You believe that there is one God. Good! Even the demons believe that—and shudder." Mere intellectual "belief" is not what the Bible means by the word *faith*. The Greek words translated *belief* and *faith* mean to *trust* and have *confidence* in someone or something.

Those who have truly believed in Christ have placed their confidence or trust in Him and His perfect life and work to *bring and sustain them* in an eternal relationship with God. And such confidence in Christ cannot help but change a person's life. A simple phrase clarifies the point: you are saved by faith alone but saving faith is never alone! It is in the nature of true faith in God to believe in His Son and love His people. If we see neither of these in a person's life we have to question if they genuinely know God (or we might better say if they are truly known *by* God). Such a person's faith is dead in James' thinking.

Does that mean we have to believe or love perfectly? No! We are not meant to base our confidence before God on how well we do but on how well Christ does. Don't fall into the performance trap of thinking you have never done enough. Just ask yourself: Do I believe that Jesus is alive, resurrected from the dead, and know that I am called to care for my brothers and sisters in Christ?

CORRELATION

And this is his command: to believe in the name of his Son, Jesus Christ, and to love one another as he commanded us. The one who keeps God's commands lives in him, and he in them. And this is how we know that he lives in us: We know it by the Spirit he gave us.

1 John 3:23-24

RECITATION

I believe in God the Father, Almighty Maker of heaven and earth.

And in Jesus Christ his only Son our Lord; who was conceived by the Holy Spirit,

born of the Virgin Mary, suffered under Pontius Pilate, was crucified, dead, and buried; he descended into hell; the third day he rose again from the dead;

He ascended into heaven, and sits on the right hand of God the Father Almighty; from there he shall come to judge the living and the dead.

I believe in the Holy Spirit; the holy Christian Church; the communion of saints; the forgiveness of sins; the resurrection of the body; and the life everlasting. AMEN.

The Apostle's Creed

APPLICATION

What has come to mind, either through the passage or in your reflection that you want to remember?

Love One Another

Passage: 1 John 3:11-4:21

Meditation: 1 John 4:2-21
Pause and Reflect Silently
Highlight Key Phrases
Look to and Lift up Christ

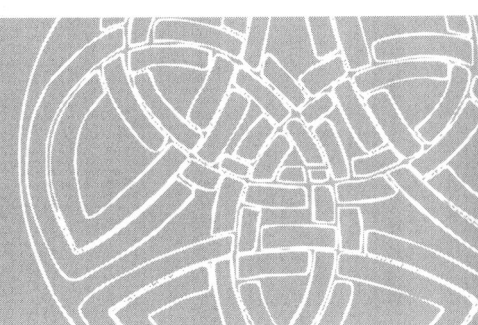

²This is how you can recognize the Spirit of God: Every spirit that acknowledges that Jesus Christ has come in the flesh is from God, ³but every spirit that does not acknowledge Jesus is not from God. This is the spirit of the antichrist, which you have heard is coming and even now is already in the world.

⁴You, dear children, are from God and have overcome them, because the one who is in you is greater than the one who is in the world.

⁵They are from the world and therefore speak from the viewpoint of the world, and the world listens to them.

⁶We are from God, and whoever knows God listens to us; but whoever is not from God does not listen to us. This is how we recognize the Spirit of truth and the spirit of falsehood.

⁷Dear friends, let us love one another, for love comes from God. Everyone who loves has been born of God and knows God.

⁸Whoever does not love does not know God, because God is love.

⁹This is how God showed his love among us: He sent his one and only Son into the world that we might live through him. ¹⁰This is love: not that we loved God, but that he loved us and sent his Son as an atoning sacrifice for our sins. ¹¹Dear friends, since God so loved us, we also ought to love one another. ¹²No one has ever seen God; but if we love one another, God lives in us and his love is made complete in us.

¹³This is how we know that we live in him and he in us: He has given us of his Spirit. ¹⁴And we have seen and testify that the Father has sent his Son to be the Savior of the world. ¹⁵If anyone acknowledges that Jesus is the Son of God, God lives in them and they in God. ¹⁶And so we know and rely on the love God has for us.

God is love. Whoever lives in love lives in God, and God in them. ¹⁷This is how love is made complete among us so that we will have confidence on the day of judgment: In this world we are like Jesus. ¹⁸There is no fear in love. But perfect love drives out fear, because fear has to do with punishment. The one who fears is not made perfect in love.

¹⁹We love because he first loved us. ²⁰Whoever claims to love God yet hates a brother or sister is a liar. For whoever does not love their brother and sister, whom they have seen, cannot love God, whom they have not seen. ²¹And he has given us this command: Anyone who loves God must also love their brother and sister.

REFLECTION

We finish our devotional with John's thoughts on brotherly love and the Revelation he received on the island of Patmos.

The Apostle John was unique among the Apostles. He seems to have had an anger problem (Luke 9:54) but he became known as the Apostle of love. He probably was Jesus' closest friend but he became neither the primary spokesman for the faith (Peter, Paul) nor the leader of the Jerusalem church (James, the brother of Jesus). *But* we have five New Testament books written by him (his Gospel, 3 letters and the Book of Revelation) which have had a profound impact on the church and world for centuries.

Our devotional in James gives us a good background on this reading. John, too, is concerned that we have a well-founded assurance of our salvation. We need an inner sense of confidence in God to be able to handle the challenges and hardships of this world. How do we develop this inner quality? By loving God's people and trusting in His Son. John makes this point over and over again in his letters and writings. It really is that simple.

There are challenging truths and enduring questions we have of our faith and the nature of God and eternity, but John embodies the KISS principle for the Christian life: Keep It Simple, Saint! Love your brothers and sisters, put your confidence in Christ, and wait eagerly for his coming as the Savior and Lord of mankind!

Being simple does not make it easy though. To make our faith in Christ and our love for other Christians the center of our lives will take great effort, sacrifice, time and wisdom. We need to reorder our hearts and lives and leave behind patterns of thinking and relating that we might have taken decades developing. And we will have to "neglect" old pursuits in our life to find the time to learn these new habits. Which ones need to be left behind? That is between you and God: Are you ready to ask and let go?

CORRELATION

I write these things to you who believe in the name of the Son of God so that you may know that you have eternal life. This is the confidence we have in approaching God: that if we ask anything according to his will, he hears us.
            1 John 5:13-14

So do not worry, saying, 'What shall we eat?' or 'What shall we drink?' or 'What shall we wear?' For the pagans run after all these things, and your heavenly Father knows that you need them. But seek first his kingdom and his righteousness, and all these things will be given to you as well.
            Matthew 6:31-33

RECITATION

O Father, light up
   the small duties of this day's life;

May they shine
   with the beauty of Your countenance.

May we believe that glory can dwell
   in the commonest task of every day.

Augustine of Hippo

APPLICATION

What has come to mind, either through the passage or in your reflection that you want to remember?

A Voice and a Vision

Passage: Revelation 1:1-20

Meditation: Revelation 1:1-20
Pause and Reflect Silently
Highlight Key Phrases
Look to and Lift up Christ

¹*The revelation from Jesus Christ, which God gave him to show his servants what must soon take place. He made it known by sending his angel to his servant John,* ²*who testifies to everything he saw—that is, the word of God and the testimony of Jesus Christ.* ³*Blessed is the one who reads aloud the words of this prophecy, and blessed are those who hear it and take to heart what is written in it, because the time is near.*

⁴*John, To the seven churches in the province of Asia: Grace and peace to you from him who is, and who was, and who is to come, and from the seven spirits before his throne,* ⁵*and from Jesus Christ, who is the faithful witness, the firstborn from the dead, and the ruler of the kings of the earth. To him who loves us and has freed us from our sins by his blood,* ⁶*and has made us to be a kingdom and priests to serve his God and Father—to him be glory and power for ever and ever! Amen.*

⁷*"Look, he is coming with the clouds," and "every eye will see him, even those who pierced him"; and all peoples on earth "will*

mourn because of him." So shall it be! Amen. ⁸"I am the Alpha and the Omega," says the Lord God, "who is, and who was, and who is to come, the Almighty."

⁹I, John, your brother and companion in the suffering and kingdom and patient endurance that are ours in Jesus, was on the island of Patmos because of the word of God and the testimony of Jesus. ¹⁰On the Lord's Day I was in the Spirit, and I heard behind me a loud voice like a trumpet, ¹¹which said: "Write on a scroll what you see and send it to the seven churches: to Ephesus, Smyrna, Pergamum, Thyatira, Sardis, Philadelphia and Laodicea."

¹²I turned around to see the voice that was speaking to me. And when I turned I saw seven golden lampstands, ¹³and among the lampstands was someone like a son of man, dressed in a robe reaching down to his feet and with a golden sash around his chest. ¹⁴The hair on his head was white like wool, as white as snow, and his eyes were like blazing fire. ¹⁵His feet were like bronze glowing in a furnace, and his voice was like the sound of rushing waters. ¹⁶In his right hand he held seven stars, and coming out of his mouth was a sharp, double-edged sword. His face was like the sun shining in all its brilliance. ¹⁷When I saw him, I fell at his feet as though dead. Then he placed his right hand on me and said: "Do not be afraid. I am the First and the Last. ¹⁸I am the Living One; I was dead, and now look, I am alive for ever and ever! And I hold the keys of death and Hades. ¹⁹"Write, therefore, what you have seen, what is now and what will take place later.

[20] *The mystery of the seven stars that you saw in my right hand and of the seven golden lampstands is this: The seven stars are the angels of the seven churches, and the seven lampstands are the seven churches.*

REFLECTION

Jesus' life inspires us with his insight, compassion, and courage. His relationship with his Heavenly Father reassures us that God is worth all the sweat, loss and suffering in this life. If Jesus was willing to die in obedience to him, he must be truly wonderful!

As we come to know and admire Jesus in his earthly life, though, we need to be careful not to stop at the Resurrection in our understanding of him. He is no longer a Suffering Servant: He is now the exalted Lord of the Universe, supremely powerful, having all authority in heaven and on earth. No one or no thing can stand before him!

Revelation (notice it is not *revelations*) gives us this bigger picture of Christ and of life that we desperately need. We miss the point of the book if we do not see that it is about the glorified Word of God, Jesus Christ himself, and not primarily about what the sixth seal or third trumpet mean.

Revelation was not written to frighten us but to inspire us. We're to be blessed not disheartened as we read it. There are a lot of scary things in this world but we come to see that they are ultimately all under the authority of and within the plan of our Lord and Savior, Jesus Christ.

John received these visions on the island of Patmos. He was most likely there as a prisoner for his faith but it may be, simply, that he was there to preach. While there he had an unexpected encounter with the glorified Christ.

John's vision gives us a picture of Jesus as an exalted, Divine High Priest, who is both ministering before God *for* us, and ministering for God *to us*. He will continue to faithfully do both throughout this age. Christ commissioned John as a prophet to speak to His church.

CORRELATION

"Do not be afraid. I am the First and the Last. I am the Living One; I was dead, and now look, I am alive forever and ever! And I hold the keys of death and Hades.

Revelation 1:17b-18

RECITATION

LORD, MAKE ME AN INSTRUMENT OF YOUR PEACE,

where there is hatred, let me sow love,

where there is injury, pardon,

where there is discord, may I bring harmony,

where there is error, may I bring truth,

where there is doubt, may I bring faith,

where there is despair, may I bring hope,

where there is darkness, may I bring light,

and where there is sadness, may I bring joy.

O Divine Master,

grant that I may not so much seek

To be consoled, as to console,

to be understood, as to understand,

to be loved, as to love.

for it is in giving that we receive;

it is in pardoning that we are pardoned;

and it is in dying that we are born into eternal life.

Francis of Assisi

APPLICATION

What has come to mind, either through the passage or in your reflection that you want to remember?

Messages to the Churches

Passage: Revelation 2:1-3:22

Meditation: Revelation 2:18-3:6
Pause and Reflect Silently
Highlight Key Phrases
Look to and Lift up Christ

18 "To the angel of the church in Thyatira write: These are the words of the Son of God, whose eyes are like blazing fire and whose feet are like burnished bronze. 19I know your deeds, your love and faith, your service and perseverance, and that you are now doing more than you did at first.

20Nevertheless, I have this against you: You tolerate that woman Jezebel, who calls herself a prophet. By her teaching she misleads my servants into sexual immorality and the eating of food sacrificed to idols. 21I have given her time to repent of her immorality, but she is unwilling. 22So I will cast her on a bed of suffering, and I will make those who commit adultery with her suffer intensely, unless they repent of her ways. 23I will strike her children dead. Then all the churches will know that I am he who searches hearts and minds, and I will repay each of you according to your deeds.

24Now I say to the rest of you in Thyatira, to you who do not hold to her teaching and have not learned Satan's so-called deep secrets, 'I will not impose any other burden on you, ²⁵except to hold on to what you have until I come.'

²⁶To the one who is victorious and does my will to the end, I will give authority over the nations—²⁷that one 'will rule them with an iron scepter and will dash them to pieces like pottery'—just as I have received authority from my Father. ²⁸I will also give that one the morning star. ²⁹Whoever has ears, let them hear what the Spirit says to the churches.

3¹To the angel of the church in Sardis write: These are the words of him who holds the seven spirits of God and the seven stars. I know your deeds; you have a reputation of being alive, but you are dead. ²Wake up! Strengthen what remains and is about to die, for I have found your deeds unfinished in the sight of my God.

³Remember, therefore, what you have received and heard; hold it fast, and repent. But if you do not wake up, I will come like a thief, and you will not know at what time I will come to you.

⁴Yet you have a few people in Sardis who have not soiled their clothes. They will walk with me, dressed in white, for they are worthy. ⁵The one who is victorious will, like them, be dressed in white. I will never blot out the name of that person from the book of life, but will acknowledge that name before my Father and his angels. ⁶Whoever has ears, let them hear what the Spirit says to the churches.

REFLECTION

Nothing in this world will ever be everything we hope it to be. Even "perfect" moments in life pass and we find ourselves having to face another day in a frustrating, demanding, chaotic world filled with never-ending conflicts.

When we turn our attention to the "church" we may find ourselves with mixed feelings too. It has so much potential to change the world but it gets sidelined by controversies and compromises. Some churches slide into the prevailing immorality of their time while others become so rigid that you are not accepted unless you dress like it was the 1950's.

If you are idealistic and long to see the church be everything it could be, you need to take to heart what Jesus says to *his* church in Revelation. To understand his message we need to start with the meaning of the number 7. Revelation is filled with significant numbers: 3, 4, 10, 12, but the most significant number in the book is 7. There are at least 19 different sets of "7's." John's letter to the 7 churches in Asia Minor is the first specifically mentioned. It has been thought to refer to the concepts of "essence," "perfection," or "completion."[21]

If the significance of the number 7 is that of *essence* it would mean that the number refers to the way something really is. The 7 letters, then, reveal the *real church* in all of its strengths and weaknesses. These 7 churches are not just first century churches randomly chosen by Jesus, but are representative of His church as it was then and how it will often be throughout the centuries.

Christ's messages expose how messy, imperfect and misguided churches can get. But they also reveal that they're being guided, corrected and encouraged by their Head, Jesus Christ. There's an old saying: do not let the perfect become the enemy of the good. Our idealism can become a problem if we expect churches to be perfect without "spot or blemish."

Just about every church will have strengths we need to appreciate and problems we need to address. Notice, too, that size and reputation have little to do with Christ's approval, and every church is challenged to stay true to Christ to receive His heavenly reward.

CORRELATION

To the angel of the church in Philadelphia write: These are the words of him who is holy and true, who holds the key of David. What he opens no one can shut, and what he shuts no one can open.
Revelation 3:7

RECITATION

Thanks be to you, our Lord Jesus Christ,

For all the benefits you have given us,

For all the pains and insults you have borne for us.

Most merciful Redeemer, Friend, and Brother,

May we know you more clearly,

Love you more dearly,

And follow you more nearly:

Forever and ever. AMEN.

Richard Chichester

APPLICATION

What has come to mind, either through the passage or in your reflection that you want to remember?

The Throne Room of Heaven

Passage: Revelation 4:1-7:17

Meditation: Revelation 4:1-5:5
Pause and Reflect Silently
Highlight Key Phrases
Look to and Lift up Christ

¹*After this I looked, and there before me was a door standing open in heaven. And the voice I had first heard speaking to me like a trumpet said, "Come up here, and I will show you what must take place after this." ²At once I was in the Spirit, and there before me was a throne in heaven with someone sitting on it.*

³*And the one who sat there had the appearance of jasper and ruby. A rainbow that shone like an emerald encircled the throne. ⁴Surrounding the throne were twenty-four other thrones, and seated on them were twenty-four elders. They were dressed in white and had crowns of gold on their heads. ⁵From the throne came flashes of lightning, rumblings and peals of thunder. In front of the throne, seven lamps were blazing. These are the seven spirits of God. ⁶Also in front of the throne there was what looked like a sea of glass, clear as crystal.*

In the center, around the throne, were four living creatures, and they were covered with eyes, in front and in back. ⁷The first living creature was like a lion, the second was like an ox, the third had a face like a man, the fourth was like a flying eagle. ⁸Each of the four living creatures had six wings and was covered with eyes all around, even under its wings. Day and night they never stop saying: "'Holy, holy, holy is the Lord God Almighty,' who was, and is, and is to come."

⁹Whenever the living creatures give glory, honor and thanks to him who sits on the throne and who lives forever and ever, ¹⁰the twenty-four elders fall down before him who sits on the throne and worship him who lives forever and ever. They lay their crowns before the throne and say:

¹¹"You are worthy, our Lord and God, to receive glory and honor and power, for you created all things, and by your will they were created and have their being."

5:¹Then I saw in the right hand of him who sat on the throne a scroll with writing on both sides and sealed with seven seals. ²And I saw a mighty angel proclaiming in a loud voice, "Who is worthy to break the seals and open the scroll?" ³But no one in heaven or on earth or under the earth could open the scroll or even look inside it. ⁴I wept and wept because no one was found who was worthy to open the scroll or look inside. ⁵Then one of the elders said to me, "Do not weep! See, the Lion of the tribe of Judah, the Root of David, has triumphed. He is able to open the scroll and its seven seals."

REFLECTION

If we put ourselves back into the historical moment of the first readers of Revelation we would have been able to look back on centuries of recorded Scripture and yet have little or no idea what heaven was really like.

The Lord God Almighty had come into our realm and revealed aspects of His glory and life. He revealed Himself in Jerusalem's temple (Isaiah 6) and in the "sky" above Babylon (Ezekiel 1), giving us glimpses of His throne and the creatures who surround Him. Daniel was given a significant glimpse into heaven in one of his visions (Daniel 7:9-10)

But it is not until this moment in Revelation that we actually pass over into God's realm and see some of what awaits us. And what does? A world filled with wonders and exotic creatures dominated by a Being who is Infinite, Eternal, and Overwhelmingly Glorious. Everything centers on him. Everything bows before him. Everything serves his purposes. *And everything is at peace.*

One commentator wrote that John was summoned into the "Supreme Headquarters" to re-gain a heavenly view of the spiritual war that the Christians were then in the middle of. What does he see? Heaven is filled with a multitude beyond number who are engrossed in worshiping God as the Creator (Ch 4). And that worship is surpassed only by the arrival of the glorified Lamb who takes his place as the Supreme Ruler and Redeemer of mankind (Ch 5).

The Heavenly Worship Service leads into the next series of 7's: the 7 Seals. If the 7 Letters revealed the *real Church*, the 7 Seals reveal the *real Ruler* behind the cataclysms that shake the earth. As the Seals are opened we find ourselves asking question after question. What is in the scroll? What are the four horsemen of the Apocalypse? When does this happen? All of these questions are natural and fascinating. As we seek to answer them for ourselves, though, we need to maintain our sense of awe and humility before the commanding, magnificent, astonishing picture it gives of Christ.

CORRELATION

> *Then the kings of the earth, the princes, the generals, the rich, the mighty, and everyone else, both slave and free, hid in caves and among the rocks of the mountains. They called to the mountains and the rocks, "Fall on us and hide us from the face of him who sits on the throne and from the wrath of the Lamb!*
>
> Revelation 6:15-16

RECITATION

Lord, whatever this day may bring

Your name be praised.

Be gracious to me and help me.

Grant me strength to bear whatever you may send,
 and let not fear overrule me.

I trust your grace and commit my life wholly into your
 hands.

Whether I live or whether I die, I am with you.

And you are with me,

O my Lord and my God.

Lord, I wait for your salvation,
 and for the coming of your kingdom. AMEN.

Dietrich Bonhoeffer

APPLICATION

What has come to mind, either through the passage or in your reflection that you want to remember?

Hallelujah!

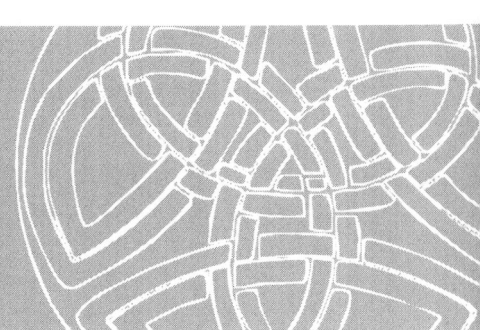

Passage: Revelation 19:1-20:15

Meditation: Revelation 20:1-15
Pause and Reflect Silently
Highlight Key Phrases
Look to and Lift up Christ

¹And I saw an angel coming down out of heaven, having the key to the Abyss and holding in his hand a great chain. ²He seized the dragon, that ancient serpent, who is the devil, or Satan, and bound him for a thousand years.

³He threw him into the Abyss, and locked and sealed it over him, to keep him from deceiving the nations anymore until the thousand years were ended. After that, he must be set free for a short time.

⁴I saw thrones on which were seated those who had been given authority to judge. And I saw the souls of those who had been beheaded because of their testimony about Jesus and because of the word of God. They had not worshiped the beast or its image and had not received its mark on their foreheads or their hands. They came to life and reigned with Christ a thousand years.

⁵(The rest of the dead did not come to life until the thousand

years were ended.) This is the first resurrection. ⁶Blessed and holy are those who share in the first resurrection. The second death has no power over them, but they will be priests of God and of Christ and will reign with him for a thousand years.

⁷When the thousand years are over, Satan will be released from his prison ⁸and will go out to deceive the nations in the four corners of the earth—Gog and Magog—and to gather them for battle. In number they are like the sand on the seashore. ⁹They marched across the breadth of the earth and surrounded the camp of God's people, the city he loves. But fire came down from heaven and devoured them. ¹⁰And the devil, who deceived them, was thrown into the lake of burning sulfur, where the beast and the false prophet had been thrown. They will be tormented day and night for ever and ever.

¹¹Then I saw a great white throne and him who was seated on it. The earth and the heavens fled from his presence, and there was no place for them. ¹²And I saw the dead, great and small, standing before the throne, and books were opened. Another book was opened, which is the book of life. The dead were judged according to what they had done as recorded in the books.

¹³The sea gave up the dead that were in it, and death and Hades gave up the dead that were in them, and each person was judged according to what they had done. ¹⁴Then death and Hades were thrown into the lake of fire. The lake of fire is the second death. ¹⁵Anyone whose name was not found written in the book of life was thrown into the lake of fire.

REFLECTION

Hallelujah is Hebrew in origin. It combines *Hallel* (= praise), *Lu* (= to), and *Yah* (= God). God revealed His personal name to Moses in the burning bush as *Yahweh*. Scholars later translated the word *Jehovah*. The Jewish people so revered God's name that they would not repeat it in full. The closest they would come to saying the personal name of God was when they proclaimed Hallelu*jah*! Praise to Yahweh!

At the moment of ultimate victory, Hallelujah will be proclaimed four times in celebration of God's ultimate victory over all of His enemies. The powers of sin, Satan and death will one day be defeated and the final word of God's people will be a resounding HALLELUJAH!

Revelation gives us a dramatic, heavenly view of events that take place between the ascension of Christ and the return of Christ. Regardless of how one decides on the timing of the Great Tribulation and Rapture of the Church, Revelation reassures us that the final outcome will be glorious!

A simple outline of Revelation goes as follows: The true ascended Master, Jesus Christ, oversees all the events of heaven and earth as Seven Letters are written; Seven Seals are opened; Seven Trumpets are blown; Seven heavenly Signs are revealed; Seven Bowls are poured out; and lastly, Seven Events climax in the Wedding Feast of Christ and His Bride. These six series of seven's give us the forward movement of history from the first century to the last century; they give us *the real story of History*!

We do not live in a cold, meaningless, self-created cosmos but in a created, guided, meaningful creation which has an all-Wise, all-Powerful, all-Loving Divine Redeemer at its center. He has been single-mindedly focused on redeeming His people and His world. And He is moving everything toward the Day when He will defeat and forever "quarantine" sin, death and Satan so that they will never again affect His plans or distress His people. HALLELUJAH!

CORRELATION

I saw heaven standing open and there before me was a white horse, whose rider is called Faithful and True. With justice he judges and wages war. His eyes are like blazing fire, and on his head are many crowns. He has a name written on him that no one knows but he himself. He is dressed in a robe dipped in blood, and his name is the Word of God. Revelation 19:11-13

RECITATION

GOD, GRANT ME THE SERENITY
   to accept the things I cannot change;

Courage to change the things I can and
   the wisdom to know the difference.

To live one day at a time;
   enjoying one moment at a time;

Accepting hardship as the pathway to peace.

To take, as He did, this sinful world as it is, not as I would have it.

Trusting that He will make all things right if I surrender to His Will.

That I may be reasonably happy in this life and supremely happy with You forever in the next. Amen

Reinhold Neibuhr

APPLICATION

What has come to mind, either through the passage or in your reflection that you want to remember?

The New Jerusalem

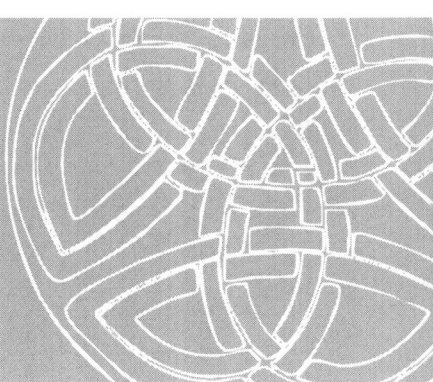

Passage: Revelation 21:1-22:21

Meditation: Revelation 21:1-14, 18-19a, 21-23
Pause and Reflect Silently
Highlight Key Phrases
Look to and Lift up Christ

¹Then I saw "a new heaven and a new earth," for the first heaven and the first earth had passed away, and there was no longer any sea. ²I saw the Holy City, the new Jerusalem, coming down out of heaven from God, prepared as a bride beautifully dressed for her husband. ³And I heard a loud voice from the throne saying, "Look! God's dwelling place is now among the people, and he will dwell with them. They will be his people, and God himself will be with them and be their God. ⁴'He will wipe every tear from their eyes. There will be no more death or mourning or crying or pain, for the old order of things has passed away."

⁵He who was seated on the throne said, "I am making everything new!" Then he said, "Write this down, for these words are trustworthy and true." ⁶He said to me: "It is done. I am the Alpha and the Omega, the Beginning and the End. To the thirsty I will give water without cost from the spring of the water of

life. ⁷*Those who are victorious will inherit all this, and I will be their God and they will be my children. ⁸But the cowardly, the unbelieving, the vile, the murderers, the sexually immoral, those who practice magic arts, the idolaters and all liars—they will be consigned to the fiery lake of burning sulfur. This is the second death."*

⁹*One of the seven angels who had the seven bowls full of the seven last plagues came and said to me, "Come, I will show you the bride, the wife of the Lamb." ¹⁰And he carried me away in the Spirit to a mountain great and high, and showed me the Holy City, Jerusalem, coming down out of heaven from God. ¹¹It shone with the glory of God, and its brilliance was like that of a very precious jewel, like a jasper, clear as crystal. ¹²It had a great, high wall with twelve gates, and with twelve angels at the gates. On the gates were written the names of the twelve tribes of Israel. ¹³There were three gates on the east, three on the north, three on the south and three on the west. ¹⁴The wall of the city had twelve foundations, and on them were the names of the twelve apostles of the Lamb.*

¹⁸*The wall was made of jasper, and the city of pure gold, as pure as glass. ¹⁹The foundations of the city walls were decorated with every kind of precious stone... ²¹The twelve gates were twelve pearls, each gate made of a single pearl. The great street of the city was of gold, as pure as transparent glass.*

²²*I did not see a temple in the city, because the Lord God Almighty and the Lamb are its temple. ²³The city does not need*

the sun or the moon to shine on it, for the glory of God gives it light, and the Lamb is its lamp.

REFLECTION

Scripture began with the creation of the heavens and earth, the presentation of the Garden of Eden and the marriage of Adam and Eve. It ends with the creation of the new heavens and earth, the presentation of the Eden-like New Jerusalem, and the marriage of Christ and His Bride. There will be a time when the events between these two bookends of human history will be a very distant memory and God's people will be wholly enjoying the glories of God in perfection.

The Apostle Paul said, "I consider that our present sufferings are not worth comparing with the glory that will be revealed in us. For the creation waits in eager expectation for the children of God to be revealed (Ro 8:18-19)." Notice Paul speaks to what will be revealed *in us* not revealed *to us*. Of all the glories that we will see one of the greatest will be what God has created us to be! Mankind is the apex of God's original creation and transformed believers will be the apex of God's new creation!

C.S. Lewis said, "It is a serious thing to live in a society of possible gods and goddesses, to remember that the dullest and most uninteresting person you can talk to may one day be a creature which, if you saw it now, you would be strongly tempted to worship, or else a horror and a corruption such as you now meet, if at all, only in a nightmare. All day long we are, in some degree, helping each other to one or the other of these destinations; there are no ordinary people. You have never talked to a mere mortal. Nations, cultures, arts, civilizations - these are mortal, and their life is to ours the life of a gnat. But it is immortals whom we joke with, work with, marry, snub, and exploit - immortal horrors or everlasting splendors."[22]

When you get discouraged or disillusioned, remind yourself of the glory to be revealed in you and to you. And say to yourself often, *"God knows what He is doing. He knows where He is going. He will bring us safely home. **And this isn't that much to ask**, in light of what He has in store for us!"*

CORRELATION

Dear friends, now we are children of God, and what we will be has not yet been made known. But we know that when Christ appears, we shall be like him, for we shall see him as he is.
1 John 3:2

RECITATION

Father, we give you thanks for all the gifts you freely bestow on us. For the beauty and wonder of your creation, in earth and sky and sea, Lord, we thank you.

For our daily food and drink, our homes and families, and our friends, Lord, we thank you.

For minds to think, and hearts to love, and hands to serve, Lord, we thank you. For health and strength to work, and leisure to rest and play, Lord, we thank you.

For the brave and courageous, who are patient in suffering and faithful in adversity, Lord, we thank you.

For the communion of saints, in all times and places, Lord, we thank you.

Above all, we give you thanks for the great mercies and promises given to us in Christ Jesus our Lord; to him be praise and glory, with you, O Father, and the Holy Spirit, now and forever. AMEN.

APPLICATION

What has come to mind, either through the passage or in your reflection that you want to remember?

ENDNOTES

1. John 14:6.

2. This process is what initiates and motivates our life-long pursuit of His kingdom and righteousness (Matt 6:33).

3. Special thanks to Pastor Mike Lacaze for giving me opportunity to write the first drafts of these reflections!

4. Dallas Willard's *Hearing God* is an excellent introduction to this area of the Christian life.

5. One long-practiced discipline in the Christian tradition is called *Lectio Divina*, which translates as "Divine Reading." I am not rigidly following the practice but am integrating its primary focus into this devotional. It is a slow, reflective way of reading Scripture which encourages a repetitive reading of a small section of a passage. It often is practiced in a four stage format of lectio (reading text), meditatio (reflection on each word or phrase), oratio (response in prayer), contemplatio (restful listening).

6. All Scripture passages are from the NIV 2011.

7. There were a number of unique Greek philosophers and philosophical schools. Yet the concept of an impersonal "rational principle" behind the universe was widely held and taught.

8. The Jewish Targums were Aramaic translations of the Hebrew Scriptures. They used the Aramaic word "Memra (i.e. word)" as a substitute for God's name. The Targums were widely used during the first century AD. Comments on the Jewish concepts of the Word are found in the article on "The Logos in John's Prologue" in the Lexham Bible Dictionary.

9. This is a prayer based on selected verses in Psalm 90 which I have personally written.

10. The Jesus Prayer has a few different forms. I have chosen to include one that includes the phrase "a sinner" on the end. Though this might raise the issue of our identity as saints as Christians, it is the most widely used form of this prayer. Sinners are what we are born as in Adam. Saints are who we are re-born as in Christ.

11. This reading of the Apostle's Creed has updated some archaic language and has had one key word changed. The traditional reading of "the holy Catholic Church" has been changed to read "the holy Christian Church" which better reflects the original intentions of the writers and avoids the confusion that might arise with the connotations of "Catholic" to non-Catholic readers.

12. Ken Gire, in *Between Heaven and Earth (San Francisco: HarperCollins, 1997) p. 168.*

13. Rick Warren, in *The Purpose Driven Life (Grand Rapids: Zondervan, 2002) p. 17.*

14. Ken Gire, *Between Heaven and Earth (San Francisco: HarperCollins, 1997) p. 145.* A concluding phrase "day by day" was added later. I have chosen to stay closer to the original.

15. Ken Gire, in *Between Heaven and Earth (San Francisco: HarperCollins, 1997), pp. 253-254.* Excerpted from the original prayer which was longer and written around Christmas 1943 from a concentration camp.

16. From The *Litany of Thanksgiving in the Book of Common Prayer (bcponline.org).*

17. Dallas Willard, in *The Divine Conspiracy (New York: HarperCollins, 1998), pp. 91-95.*

18. C.S. Lewis, in *God In The Dock: Essays on Theology and Ethics (Eerdmans, 1970)* From the essay "Christian Apologetics."

19. P Carnegie Simpson, in *The Fact of Jesus (New York: Fleming H. Revell Company, pre-1945), p. 44.*

20. C.S. Lewis, in *Mere Christianity (New York: Macmillan, 1960), p. 56.*

21. Michael Wilcock, in *The Message of Revelation (Leicester: Inter-Varsity Press, 1975), pp. 62-63.*

22. C.S. Lewis, in *The Weight Of Glory (New York: HarperCollins, 1949).*